LOOKING FOR YOUR SOUL MATE

BILL E. CARTER

WESTBOW
PRESS
A DIVISION OF THOMAS NELSON

WestBow Press books may be ordered through booksellers or by contacting:

WestBow Press
A Division of Thomas Nelson
1663 Liberty Drive
Bloomington, IN 47403
www.westbowpress.com
1-(866) 928-1240

Because of the dynamic nature of the Internet, any web addresses or links contained in this book may have changed since publication and may no longer be valid. The views expressed in this work are solely those of the author and do not necessarily reflect the views of the publisher, and the publisher hereby disclaims any responsibility for them.

Any people depicted in stock imagery provided by Thinkstock are models, and such images are being used for illustrative purposes only.

Certain stock imagery © Thinkstock.

ISBN: 978-1-4497-6241-4 (sc)
ISBN: 978-1-4497-6240-7 (e)

Library of Congress Control Number: 2012914097

Printed in the United States of America

WestBow Press rev. date: 03/13/2013

"LOOKING FOR YOUR SOUL MATE"

A RELATIONSHIP DEVELOPMENT WORK BOOK
DESIGNED TO BE USED AT HOME, CHURCH
(for single adult programs),
AND IN GROUP TEACHINGS!

THIS BOOK COULD BE USE AS AN ACTIVES
BOOK FOR SINGLES GROUPS.

AS YOU READ THROUGH THIS BOOK,
ALLOW THE TIME IT TAKES TO CHANGE ONE'S SELF.

KNOWLEDGE WILL BRING FORTH WISDOM,
AND FAITH CAN CHANGE A PERSON.

THIS BOOK WILL TAKE YOU

FROM YOUR PAST TO YOUR FUTURE!

"LOOKING FOR YOUR SOUL MATE"

INTRODUCTION

This book, **"LOOKING FOR YOUR SOUL MATE"**; is written to avoid mistakes we single adults can make in the search for our soul mate. *These subjects have been tried in our single adult ministry program. Each subject has input not only from me but from people that has shared feelings at the singles ministry program,*

"IT'S OK TO BE SINGLE".

This writing has been developed from a few years of writing, studying, and listening to people about their mistakes as single adults. I have placed key Bible verses to fit each subject to encourage you to think about yourself. The questions at the end of these subjects are designed to get you from the past to the future.

God wants all of us to have a great future!

SPECIAL THANKS
TO ALL BELOW

I know that God called me to write this book, **"LOOKING FOR YOUR SOUL MATE"**.
There are many people that have helped me to get to this point.
It was their prayers, faith and input that kept me going.

**May God bless each and every one of you**
**for believing in the needs of single adults!**

Pastor Dr. Ed Davis, my role model, Pastor and brother in Christ.
Pastor David Atherton, the encouragement of my writings and edited.
Pastor Mike Brown, A great man of faith and my spiritual brother.
Pastor Wil Beers, the one who believes in the vision I have for single adults
and gave an unknown person a chance to do God's work, a great man of faith.
Mary Salmon, the woman behind the ministry, a great sister in Christ;
she did the initial editing, proofreading, and kept me on track.
Her faith and prayer were received with Love.

Bill Carter editor and writer.
To all my brothers and sisters in Christ
that prayed for this book and our singles ministry program, thank you.
Thank you, WestBow Press,
for allowing us to be a part of your company.

Bill Carter

ABOUT THE AUTHOR
BILL CARTER

I was born in and grew up in Kentucky. I served 37 months in Iraq, as an Army Contractor. I became an Evangelist in 1996 and served in street and food ministries for over ten years. After my studies, I started to write on subjects in the Bible and have written over 325 subjects.

Being a single adult I took notice in other single adults and the issues of being single. I started studying different Christian's writings on the subject of single adults. They left out many issues that single adults create and have to face.

This inspired me to start writing about the issues of single adults and I ended up writing a series of books on relationship development. **"LOOKING FOR YOUR SOUL MATE"**, is just one of six books. After having a few broken hearts from relationships that were built on expectations and imaginations, I searched my heart for answers through prayers.

God has a way of addressing issues when we bring them to Him in prayer. I started to write out my past in a book called, **"Peace after a Broken Relationship"**, and within a 12 month time frame I had written a few more books. These books were written on relationship development subjects as workbooks.

Single adults make up 55% of the adults in America and only 10 to 15% of them go to Church. I feel this is one of the greatest mission fields in America. Keep us in prayer as we continue this ministry for single adults.

Bill Carter

LOOKING FOR YOUR SOUL MATE

By: Bill Carter ©2012

IT'S OK TO BE SINGLE

MINISTRY

RELATIONSHIP DEVELOPMENT

Index

DATING VERSUS COURTSHIP

Dating: (Short meaning) the activity of going out regularly with somebody as a social or romantic partner. (Longer meaning), Date: an appointment for specified time; *esp*: a social engagement between two people of the opposite sex with whom one has a social engagement.

Courtship: (short meaning) the act of paying attention to somebody with a view to developing a more intimate relationship. (Longer meaning) courting: to seek to gain or achieve, to seek the affections of; *esp*: to seek to win a pledge of marriage, to engage socially, leading to engagement and marriage.

Court: is a place where things are justified by law and judgment, (we do our best to have a righteous judgment).

I looked these two words up in the Webster's dictionary. There was a time when you talked to a person or took him or her out on a date (an appointment for specified time) to come to know one another. This was done over a given time. It takes time to earn trust and build friendship; without trust and friendship, how can you have a love-based relationship? **Dating has no real value of commitment; on the other hand courtship is based on commitment.**

How many people do you know who **use the word dating?** That has said they love each other within a few days (14 to 30 days)? Just to find they were never friends or never knew each other. Then the next thing you know they are broken up and hating each other, is that love; what happened to love? **There was no real commitment, just a few dates!**

Allow me to ask you this, how many times have you dated someone and within 14 to 30 days you said you love that person you were dating? Now how does the word dating affect relationship building? This is a great question that you should answer.

The dating game: Jumping from one person to the next person, (from bed to bed); with no value of love in sight. How many women have had sex thinking they gave all their love to some man? Men are full of actions, and sex without love has no meaning other than an activity. **Sex is not love nor does it build a real love based relationship. If so, why didn't you stay in love or have a relationship that grew and headed toward marriage? How many times have you had sex without being married?**

How many times have you dated and used these three words, "I love you", without any meaning or fulfillment? Before you date someone, where is it going to take you? **How dangerous is dating when it comes to getting hurt (heartbroken), or getting a sexually transmitted disease (STD)?**

When you started dating you lost sight of real companionship love and marriage. Have you even noticed? **Most people who date do not want more than sexual activities and are far from having any real commitment! They seem to date with expectation and imagination. Dating can be misleading and far from the truth! If I'm wrong, why do you hate the person you were dating and you said you loved?** Allow me to prove this point, go back to when you said you loved that person you were dating; are you friends today?

I would like to ask you to describe dating in your own words: (before you fill this in I ask that you finish reading this subject. _____

_____

_____

_____

_____

_____

_____

_____

_____

_____

_____

_____

Courtship: is done with all due respect of the other person, to engage socially leading to engagement and marriage. Sex is not required here, but trust and friendship are. Time is also required here, because the two of you are building a relationship to judge if this relationship could have a companionship-based love that heads toward marriage. It takes a lot of time to build companionship love.

Perhaps companionship love is another statement that you are not aware of. Does that surprise you? If we allow satan to take away the values of love, what kind of social or romantic partner will we have?

Companionship love, comes after the two of you are married in the unity structure of God's plan for marriage. That is why courtship is, and always has been, the direction we should take to build trust, friendship and love. In courting, you are building a relationship, not taking advantage of one another. In courting, we do not say "I love you" until we realize we have grown in love versus fallen in love.

How long does it take to build trust in someone you do not know, two weeks or months? How long does it take to become friends? How can you say you love someone and not know if you can trust him or her? In courting, you are doing just that, building a relationship with someone whom you can trust and love.

Courtship does not mean you have to spend every night or day with him or her. This does not give you ownership of the other person either. You have no right to place titles on a person until you can say the words "wife" or "husband". Courtship is not about having a boyfriend or girlfriend *(these two titles play no role in courtship).*

How can you say "I'm his or her boyfriend or girlfriend"? This has no value at all. Allow me to prove this. I thought you were an adult, so why are you still being a boy or a girl? So we need to mature up in reality of the responsibilities that we as Christians live in. This is God's plan that we live like Christians and learn to love as He teaches us in His word.

I would like to ask you to describe courting in your own words: _____

_____

_____

_____

_____

_____

_____

_____

_____

_____

_____

_____

I would like to ask you to describe the benefits of Courtship:_____

_____

_____

_____

_____

_____

_____

_____

_____

_____

_____

_____

I would like to ask you to describe the benefits of Dating:_____

_____

_____

_____

_____

_____

_____

_____

_____

_____

_____

_____

I hope the next time you say these three words, "I love you", you should really mean it! What is love? There are two types of love, one that is of the flesh and one that is of God or Christianity!

Now let's look at these three words (Eros, Philia and Agape) from a Christian point of view.

Eros: It is inspired by the biological structure of human nature (man and woman). The husband and wife, in a good marriage, will love each other romantically and erotically forever! Eros is the love, sexual love. This type of love should be handled in a Christian way. *(In marriage!)*

Philia: In a good marriage the husband and wife are also friends. It's a best friend relationship. This type of friendship means companionship, communication and cooperation. *(Everyday!)* Philia is family love. This is where brotherly love comes from.

Agape: Unconditional love, self-giving love, gift of love, the love that goes on loving. Even when love, becomes unlovable. I believe Agape love is not just something that happens to you; it's something you make happen. This is a gift of love. God, Himself, showed this unconditional love. We share this love by faith and by God's spirit. Agape love will grow in a real relationship and marriage. That's why we should grow in love, not fall in love!

If people would take these three words, (Eros, Philia and Agape) and make them into a three cord rope to make their love stronger, their love would last a lifetime! If companions would put forth efforts purposely to increase Philia and Agape love, this alone would increase their Eros love. This is when Eros love will flourish if properly nurtured.

If people, would increase the area of Eros love, this will reinforce the Philia and Agape love. Now you see why the three strand cord of love will last a lifetime in a marriage! These three types of love will keep and save your companionship! During courtship there is no sexual activity! Sex before marriage only blinds two people from the truth or their relationship growth!

Love will die when you spend little or no time together or when you stop sharing activities that are mutually enjoyed; remember this! Love is created or destroyed if there are or aren't pleasurable activities over a period of time. So stay involved by interacting with each other. Don't let your love die. This is your responsibility! **If couples don't reinforce their love, it will just die.**

Real love requires the ability to put yourself in your companion's place, so you will understand the differences of his or her personality. To understand and resolve these differences, through the sharing of your deepest feelings, concerns, attitudes and ideals, is a fundamental component of real love, companionship and marriage!

Now, do you know what love is about?
If everyone could write their statement of love like this,
I believe their love would be a love for a lifetime!

Proverbs 18:22
Whoso findeth a wife findeth a good thing, and obtaineth favor of the LORD.

Hebrews 13:4
Marriage is honourable in all, and the bed undefiled:

Is dating wrong? No, we make it wrong!
Is courtship wrong? No, it leads to the truth!

Notes: _____

_____

_____

_____

_____

_____

_____

_____

_____

_____

_____

_____

_____

HOW TO FIND YOUR SOUL MATE

For all single adults who have been seeking to find their soul mate, I've got great news for you. God does not create soul mates! *This would take away the free will that God gave to men and women!* God has a marriage plan that He formed in unity with His love toward us! I want you to be honest here in this passage that I am writing to all single adults. I want you to think about an answer for this question that I'm addressing to you today. **Do you have free will?** Take more than a few moments to think about your free will. *Most people forget that God gave each one of us free will. Why did God give us free will during the creation of mankind? God did not believe in bondage.* But, it is true that God is our creator; if you are a Christian you must know or believe this. (Read Gen. 2)

The question still remains; do you have free will?

I need you to answer this question, before you read further into this book.

If I could get you to understand that there is no soul mate until a bond has been created through marriage; on behalf of God's, unity structure of marriage. This alone would bring forth a blessing in the development of companionship love. With all that I know and have been blessed with. I want to reveal something that God woke me up today at 4:30 in the morning to add to this book called, "Looking for Your Soul Mate." Open up your heart and mind and allow yourself to receive this information that can and will bless you as a single adult.

In order to have a companion or to have someone you love, you must be aware of the facts. *Anyone who falls in love can and for the most part will fall out of love.* Why is this? They use the word "fall."

Fall: *to come down freely from a higher to a lower position, moved by the force of gravity, to drop or be dropped or lowered, to drop or come down suddenly from an upright position, especially by accident.* **To become lower or be reduced in amount, value, or quality!**

People that allow love to grow will develop the time and stages of growth that is needed to have companionship love. This is where we have a foundation of love!

Grow: *intransitive verb to become larger in size through* **natural development,** *intransitive verb to expand or become more developed or intense, intransitive verb to be capable of developing* **naturally and remaining in a naturally healthy state,** *intransitive verb to* **move from one condition to another, especially gradually!**

We must meet in order to come to know each other.
There must be an attraction to go to the next steps.
One of the two will ask the other out.
We must allow time to pass to come to know each other.
We must develop a type of friendship first,
in order to start to trust one another.
With time and trust, we develop a greater trust and then a great friendship.
The trust that is grown from friendship,
will allow the time it takes to grow in love.
As love grows so will a greater trust.
Courtship develops here.
It's through courtship that people tend to become engaged to be married.
Marriage comes after the time of growth.
Before marriage, the two of you
need to receive counseling from a Pastor!
Pastors are a part of God's unity structure.
Without counseling, you may become foolish!
The last thing you need as a spouse is a foolish marriage!
In marriage, you have companionship love.
Companionship love develops and creates our soul mate!
This is done by God's unity structure of marriage.
This is where we get the word, "soul mate"!

I want to ask you just a few questions:

1: Do you have free will? Yes or no

2: Did you fall in love? Yes or no

3: Did you grow in love? Yes or no

4: Which is better and will last a life time?

    a: To Grow in love
    b: Companionship love
    c: To have God's unity structure of love in marriage
    d: All of the above

5: Which is better, to fall in love or to grow in love?

    a: Fall in love
    b: Grow in love

6: Does God create a soul mate?

   a: yes   b: no

7: God gave people free will!

   a: True   b: False

8: Does God have a unity structure for love?

   a: True   b: False

9: When did God give us free will?

   a: yesterday
   b: never
   c: I don't know
   d: at creation

10: Without marriage counseling from a Pastor of your home church. What will happen to your marriage?

   a: Marriage will last
   b: You can figure it out on your own
   c: It will be much harder
   d: I do not need marriage counseling

11: Before you get married, would you seek marriage counseling from a Pastor of your home church? a: yes   b: no

12: Without marriage counseling, in your own words, what hardship will you face?

_____

_____

_____

_____

_____

_____

_____

_____

_____

_____

_____

13: Which is greater to you?

     a: to fall in love
     b: to grow in love
     c: to have companionship love
     d: to understand God's unity structure of love and marriage

14: Can you love someone enough to forgive him or her on a daily basis?

     a: yes b: no

15: If you were to get married, how important would a home church be to you? In your own words, write a small statement about why a home church would be important to you.

_____

_____

_____

_____

_____

_____

_____

_____

_____

_____

_____

_____

_____

_____

_____

_____

_____

_____

_____

_____

_____

_____

_____

_____

_____

ALLOW ME TO GIVE YOU SOME VERSES ON MARRIAGE

Genesis 2:18-25 (KJV) **18 And the LORD God said, *It is* not good that the man should be alone; I will make him an help meet for him.** 19 And out of the ground the LORD God formed every beast of the field, and every fowl of the air; and brought *them* unto Adam to see what he would call them: and whatsoever Adam called every living creature, that *was* the name thereof. 20 And Adam gave names to all cattle, and to the fowl of the air, and to every beast of the field; **but for Adam there was not found a help meet for him.**

In verse 18, we see the phrase, **"help meet"**; which means "helper comparable to him or to man".

The making of woman and the institution of marriage

21 And the LORD God caused a deep sleep to fall upon Adam, and he slept: and he took one of his ribs, and closed up the flesh instead thereof; 22 And the rib, which the LORD God had taken from man, made he a woman, and brought her unto the man. 23 And Adam said, This *is* now bone of my bones, and flesh of my flesh: she shall be called Woman, because she was taken out of Man. 24 Therefore shall a man leave his father and his mother, and shall cleave unto his wife: and they shall be one flesh. 25 And they were both naked, the man and his wife, and were not ashamed.

Proverbs 18:22 (KJV) 22 *Whoso* findeth a wife findeth a good *thing*, and obtaineth favour of the LORD.

2 Corinthians 6:11-18 (KJV) 11 O *ye* Corinthians, our mouth is open unto you, our heart is enlarged. 12 Ye are not straitened in us, but ye are straitened in your own bowels. 13 Now for a recompence in the same, (I speak as unto *my* children,) be ye also enlarged. **14 Be ye not unequally yoked together with unbelievers: for what fellowship hath righteousness with unrighteousness? And what communion hath light with darkness?** 15 And what concord hath Christ with Belial? or what part hath he that believeth with an infidel? 16 And what agreement hath the temple of God with idols? For ye are the temple of the living God; as God hath said, I will dwell in them, and walk in *them*; and I will be their God, and they shall be My people. **17 Wherefore come out from among them, and be ye separate, saith the Lord, and touch not the unclean *thing*; and I will receive you, 18 And will be a Father unto you, and ye shall be My sons and daughters, saith the Lord Almighty.**

Ecclesiastes 9:9 (KJV) ⁹ Live joyfully with the wife whom thou lovest all the days of the life of thy vanity, which He hath given thee under the sun, all the days of thy vanity: for that *is* thy portion in *this* life, and in thy labour which thou takest under the sun.

1: Should Christians be unequally yoked together with unbelievers?

    a: yes b: no

2: What is an unbeliever?

    a: not a Christian
    b: someone whose teaching is far from God's truth
    c: someone who believes they don't need a Pastor or a home church
    d: all the above

3: What does the phrase, "help meet" mean?

_____
_____
_____
_____
_____
_____
_____
_____
_____
_____
_____
_____
_____
_____

4: Therefore, shall a man leave his father and his mother, and shall cleave unto his wife: and they shall be one flesh? a: true b: false

5: And the LORD God caused a deep sleep to fall upon Adam, and he slept: and he took one of his ribs, and closed up the flesh instead thereof; And the rib, which the LORD God had taken from man, made He a woman, and brought her unto the man. What did Adam say when God did this? And Adam said, _____

_____
_____
_____
_____
_____
_____
_____

6: When a man finds a wife, does he obtain favor from the Lord?

    a: yes b: no

7: For what fellowship hath righteousness with unrighteousness? And what communion hath light with darkness? In your own words, what do these two questions mean to you?

_____

_____

_____

_____

_____

_____

_____

_____

_____

_____

_____

8: "Wherefore come out from among them, and be ye separate, saith the Lord, and touch not the unclean *thing*; and I will receive you, And will be a Father unto you, and ye shall be My sons and daughters, saith the Lord Almighty." *Do you believe these verses?*

    a: yes b: no

9: Can you live joyfully with your wife or husband?

    a: yes b: no

BE YE NOT UNEQUALLY YOKED TOGETHER WITH UNBELIEVERS

This title said it all. If you would take a look at the words unequally yoked and unbelievers. These three words will allow commitment to grow toward trust, friendship, love and companionship love marriage. The title of this subject can be found in the Bible.

2 Corinthians 6:14 Be ye not unequally yoked together with unbelievers: for what fellowship hath righteousness with unrighteousness? And what communion hath light with darkness?

This is an important verse, and I will spend some time here with the hope that you will see the truth.

Unequally: *not measurably the same, e.g. in size or number, not of the same social position, not of the same status, and rank, not evenly matched in competition, not evenly matched in education, strength, willpower, motivation, attitude, religion, spirituality, companionship, understanding, forgiveness, trust, goals, activities, food, character, people skills, managing oneself, outlook, improvements and one's life (this list could go on and on). Uneven or variable in quality or character, asymmetric, not evenly balanced, having less than the required ability to do something, unequal to the task, somebody or something not equal to another.* **Note: please understand this definition. This is part of the foundation of companionship!**

Yoked: *This is a term that is used for animal harness; it is an old word that has a lot of meaning. Frame together to become one: Two people must be equal when they are framed together, the word harness means to fit around something or with this passage two people must equally fit into this harness of life – so when they walk it does not wear on the other person; (this is where we get conflict). This is also how God sees us join together- this is the male and female psychological, physical, health and sexual part of companionship. This allows two to carry the loads of life and living together. A fitted part of the garment (yoke). This is where male and female are dressed alike, from their feet to the top of their heads – it takes time to address this type of team efforts this is growing together with understanding! Restrictive burden, something that is felt to be oppressive and restrictive – this shows that it is required that male and female must be equally yoked. A bond or tie that keeps male and female together – the yoke of marriage! Crossed spears: an archway made of crossed spears under which defeated enemies of the ancient Romans were forced to march – this is the glue of marriage to protect one another in* *temptation, sickness, future, and against all evil! Cathode ray device: electronics a device attached to the neck of a cathode ray tube to control the scanning motion of the*

These examples are real in a marriage that should always be yoked together. **Another piece of the foundation of marriage and companionship! Yoke together is for life, and if you cannot make this a real commitment, you do not need to think about marriage. There is only one true thing that will keep you yoked together, and that is the plans of marriage though God's love. Work toward the companionship love – this is where two become one. Marriage is a gift from God to man and woman; and is blessed by God. This gift will bless both the man and woman; this blessing comes from God! Make sure your marriage remains yoked together with God.**

Unbelievers: *Somebody who does not share beliefs, somebody who does not believe in an established religious faith or in conventional beliefs, does not agree in faith, does not agree with the Bible; may not be spiritual. He or she may not worship God in spirit or truth. Have no knowledge of God, Jesus, and the Holy Spirit, church or the Bible. He or she must be of the same understanding; or willing to learn the truth about God. An unbeliever only destroys the plans of God. This will also destroy your marriage.* **This warning is given by God to protect God's plan in marriage and you. Unbelievers have no faith in God or other people. They are selfish and will ignore the truth and needs of others. They make no attempt to be a team or have companionship! They will only use you and destroy you!** <u>**You must understand this!**</u>

These three words are just the first part of the verse I opened with. Now let's take a look at the second part of this verse, where the strong warning is given: ***For what fellowship hath righteousness with unrighteousness? And what communion hath light with darkness?***

Fellowship: *Sharing of experiences; a sharing of common interest, goals, experiences, or views. A group of like-minded people or companionship or friendly association.*

Similarity: membership in a group, or the sharing of characteristics with others. Like of the same faith, church, and teaching of God!

Righteousness: *(This is what Christians should understand and live by; as we seek God our Father, Jesus Christ, and the Holy Spirit. How do we worship God? We must worship God in Spirit and in truth; this is the righteousness that we as Christians should have faith in!)*

Strictly observant of morality; always behaving according to a religious or moral code. Justifiable, considered being correct. Responding to injustice; arising from the perception of great injustice or wrongdoing * righteous indignation * believing that the righteous will prevail

Unrighteousness: *Wicked; sinful or evil. Unjust; not just, fair, or right. Someone who does not believe in God, Jesus Christ, the Holy Spirit, Church and the Bible. Someone who does not worship God in spirit or truth. Someone who does not have faith as a Christian and who may worship another religion, or religions.*

Communion: ***Unity as a Christian who believes in the Trinity of God the Father, Son and the Holy Spirit; they worship God in spirit and in truth!*** *Intimacy; a feeling of emotional or spiritual closeness. Connection; a relationship, especially one in which something is communicated or shared. What communion can there be between Good and Evil?*

Light: *Jesus Christ is the light of the world. The light can be associated with Jesus being the head of the Church. Good works with the faith of God, Jesus Christ, and the Holy Spirit; being involved with our actions in faith. Good, not bad or evil!*

Darkness: *An evil force; which has no value for being a Christian. One, who does not believe in God our Father and does not worship God, does evil over good! Not a Christian.*

This verse is written to protect you and God's plans. It is when we step outside of this God given warning that we will destroy our life for a time or forever. Divorces are nothing more than a stepping stone from hell; and the plans of satan / the devil in Christianity, the enemy of God, the lord of evil, and the tempter of human beings. He is sometimes identified with Lucifer, the leader of the fallen angels.

If satan can kill the family structure; he can harm the church. Without families there will be no church. Divorces will destroy the family and churches at the same time!

Divorce is not a part of God's plans! Divorce is an un-godly act and only occurs when one or both take their eyes and heart off of God's plans. Without the light in your heart; your heart will be filled with darkness. Now I hope you see the real effects of this verse. This is only one verse that I wrote about.

If you divorce your spouse without real cause, you will face the judgment of God. You may find yourself unhappy for the rest of your life! There may be no peace, rest, sound mind, real love, companionship, trust, faith; you may just live in an empty and dark life style. These types of people always want you to take their side and view on everything! Look at the people who have had three to four marriages that they did not want to fulfill. Can you trust them? I would not. I just wrote what most pastors would not write; but it is still the truth! You will see this as you grow older, and for those who are older, give this to your friends who are seeing someone whom has been living this life-style! **Light does not need to join with darkness!**

1: (2 Corinthians 6:14), Do you understand this verse?

   a: yes b: no

2: In your own words, what does fellowship mean to you?

_____
_____
_____
_____
_____
_____
_____

3: In your own words, what does Righteousness mean to you?

_____
_____
_____
_____
_____
_____
_____

4: In your own words, what does Unrighteousness mean to you?

_____
_____
_____
_____
_____
_____
_____

5: And what communion has light with darkness; what is the light here in this question?

   a: natural light from the sun
   b: satan / devil
   c: Our Lord Jesus Christ
   d: I do not know

6: In 2 Corinthians 6:14, who does this protect?

   a: the church
   b: you
   c: Christians
   d: all the above

7: Divorces is nothing more than a stepping stone from hell and the plans of satan / the devil!

    a: disagree
    b: strongly disagree
    c: agree
    d: strongly agree

8: Dealing with question seven, why did you choose your answer?

_____

_____

_____

_____

_____

9: Satan / the devil in Christianity: is the enemy of God, the lord of evil, and the tempter of human beings. He is sometimes identified with Lucifer, the leader of the fallen angels.

    a: true b: false

MARRIAGE MATTERS

Pastor John Hagge has a book with the title *"Marriage Matters"*, and it is a great teaching as well; I suggest this book to you and yours. It is written with great detail of the Bible, and John does a real good job writing about this issue, as well.

As I write on this subject, I want you to understand that marriage does matter.

Ecclesiastes 9: 9 Live joyfully with the wife whom thou lovest all the days of the life of vanity, which he hath given thee under the sun, all the days of vanity: for that is thy portion in this life, and in thy labor which thou takest under the sun.

Look at this verse: Live joyfully with the wife thou lovest all the days of the life of vanity. This word vanity here in this verse means: to take pride and care in your marriage. Which He (God) hath given thee (you) under the sun; wives; God gave man a gift when he took on a wife. A man needs to act upon all his days of vanity; to take pride and care in his marriage. For that is thy portion in this life; as if this was a gift from God! In thy labor which thou takest under the sun; marriage is a labor of love, so have great vanity about your marriage!

Proverbs 18:22 Whoso findeth a wife findeth a good thing, and obtaineth favor of the Lord.

There is something great about marriage; two become one in the sight of God. When you are married, you should become as one with your spouse. Love is the greatest thing on earth, and a blessing that seeks to keep your marriage alive. Companionship that is, of marriage, is blessed by God, and the Lord gives you favor.

This verse in Proverbs 18:22 said that when you find a wife, you obtain favor from the Lord. This matters when you are married. Most people who are married never seek to obtain favor from the Lord! You must ask and receive this favor; one way to do this is to pray about your marriage daily. There is only one reason marriage ends in divorce. I will be repeating this statement a lot. **If your marriage is not focused on God and God's plan for marriage, it will end in divorce.**

What favor should we ask for in one's marriage? We should be asking ourselves this question, before we enter into marriage. A lot of people get married without knowledge of what God's plans are. Marriage in God's eyes is for life. There are only a few reasons to be divorced and you would need to discuss them with your pastor. Marriage counseling will open your eyes to the truth of marriage. ***Most people just go through marriage counseling to please the pastor at the church where they***

will be married. This is where failure starts; you were never focused on the gift that God gave the pastor.

If you did not receive the blessing of your pastor, you have just set up a stumbling block in your marriage! There are a lot of reasons you need to have counseling from your pastor.

The pastor is a type of protection for the family and the family in the Church. The pastor teaches, and the bigger churches have study groups for young marriages; but even in smaller Churches, the pastor should be used as a spiritual counselor. Both the men and women should know when to receive counseling; if either of the two of you ask to have counseling; both should go to counseling. This is one way to obtain favor from the Lord. I want you to know, you do not have all the answers in the adjustment time as a new couple living together. These differences that you have are real. These adjustments must be controlled, used, tried, changed, and developed; all this takes time. Remember, love is about forgiving understanding, learning and forever.

One part of a new marriage, which most people never do, is to set goals. One of your goals is to learn how you plan to handle your dissimilarities and attitudes. Getting angry is not the answer; adjustments with love are needed to allow your love, companionship and marriage to grow.

You should never have to be asked, if you know what to change and adjust!
You are adults, and you should act like it!
This is the focus of being one in marriage!
Love does change all things!
I want you to think about and write out your plan
for adjustment in the marriage you want;
because Marriage Matters.
You may need your own note book for this.

_____

_____

_____

_____

_____

_____

_____

_____

_____

_____

_____

_____

YOU AS THE MAN OR WOMAN; A COMPANION

This is where the truth needs to match the heart, mind and soul of a person who is seeking his or her soul mate. *I hope that you have read the subject of "be ye not unequally yoked together*

with unbelievers and Marriage Matters". (If not, you need to read this to help form an understanding of this subject writing.)

Now that you have read these other subjects, I hope you have found the mistakes that you have made in order to find your companion. I want you to realize that we should not live in the past and should always work toward your future. When we get single adults to take their mistakes and work toward focusing on their soul mate we see the rewards that comes out of marriage. Knowledge of the truth and focusing on your future will allow you to find your companion for life (spouse / soul mate).

But you as a man or woman need to make a greater effort in your search. This search must start with you. There are no areas of gray here; it is the truth, or it is not. If you don't include God or a Christian life style, what are you expecting? Marriage without God is like living in Hell and will head toward divorce. If you are a Christian, allow this writing to help you focus on improving yourself as a Christian. If you are not a Christian, you have a lot to work on. If you are searching for your soul mate, you have a lot of work to do, like praying for your soul mate every day, setting goals (write them out), getting out of debt, and this is where it will take time and a real effort, writing out in detail what type of soul mate you are looking for. **Do not get involved, if you are a Christian, with someone that is not a Christian. Yes he or she can become a Christian, but my question to you is will they stay focused on God's plan for marriage? This takes time to find out.**

I want to give you some real advice about getting married. If it isn't for life, what good is it? Can you and your soul mate enter into companionship love? I want to tell you something that you may not have heard. Marriage needs more than love; marriage needs companionship love! If you have not heard this, ask your pastor about companionship love that holds marriage together. **I assure you; when we have companionship love, we are in God's plans of marriage.** Pastors really need to teach this, but more so, we need to understand this subject of companionship love!

In the following subject, I will share with you more details about companionship and issues that will help you to understand and focus.

Are you willing to change your ways and life style? If not, why search for your soul mate? I will assure you this, when you meet your soul mate, you will have to grow together.

Growing means there are a lot of changes to come. If you do not believe this let me prove it. When you grew from a child to a teenager, you had to change a lot. From a teenager to an adult, more changes were needed. There are a lot of stages in being an adult. There are a lot of stages in friendship, love, companionship love and marriage. But you will never have any of these until you understand that all stages of life require us to change for the better and good of ourselves and others!

Do not become involved with a person who is not willing to change for the good of all. This is a fact of life. Those people who cannot accept changes for the good of all; end up wasting time, hurting people, never trying to help, becoming more self-centered, full of pride, never really having a relationship with God, causing more problems than they can solve, not setting goals, and for most having no future. You really need to hear me on this issue; stay away from this type of person!

This is where I'm going to step on some toes, but a little pain can cause us to learn the truth. I assure you it's all about the truth. Single adults who have been divorced will have to learn to change a lot. *There is one issue with divorced singles that stands out. They know how to get a divorce, and they keep this in their minds by choice. They form an attitude that if it doesn't work out, I will just get another divorce. Divorce people can have a mind set, ask and see if they have this type of mind set.* I aim to hit the nail really hard here. If you have been divorced and you think "if it doesn't work out I will get another divorce"; you are the type who I just wrote about. **People who think this way; need to turn their lives over to God and stop being self - centered! This mentality is self destructive! This will harm another person who is trying to be real. If you cannot change, do not seek a companion. I say that because you cannot clean up the mess you make!**

Can you be real?
Can you change?
Are you willing to give your life to God's plans?

1: We should not live in the past, but work toward the future.

   a: true b: false

2: You as a man or woman need to make a greater effort in your search. This search must start with you.

    a: disagree
    b: strongly disagree
    c: agree
    d: strongly agree

3: You must know yourself, before you come to know someone as a companion!

    a: disagree
    b: strongly disagree
    c: agree
    d: strongly agree

4: Concerning question number three, write out why you chose your answer.

_____
_____
_____
_____
_____
_____
_____
_____
_____
_____
_____
_____

5: Marriage without God is like living in Hell and will head toward divorce.

    a: disagree
    b: strongly disagree
    c: agree
    d: strongly agree

6: It would help to write out in detail what type of soul mate you are looking for.

    a: disagree
    b: strongly disagree
    c: agree
    d: strongly agree

7: I want to give you some real advice about getting married. If it isn't for life what good is it?

a: true b: false

8: Have you ever heard of companionship love?

a: yes b: no

9: Are you willing to change your ways and life style? If not, why search for your soul mate?

a: disagree
b: strongly disagree
c: agree
d: strongly agree

10: Growing means there is a lot of change to come.

a: true b: false

11: Do not become involved with a person who is not willing to change for the good of all.

a: disagree
b: strongly disagree
c: agree
d: strongly agree

12: What is going to happen, if you are the person, or you have been dating a person, who is not willing to grow or change?

_____
_____
_____
_____
_____
_____
_____
_____
_____
_____
_____
_____

13: There is one issue with divorced singles that stands out. They know how to get a divorce and they keep this in their mind by choice. They form an attitude that if it doesn't work out, I will just get another divorce.

a: disagree
b: strongly disagree
c: agree
d: strongly agree

14: In divorce, when you mess up someone's life, do you believe you can fix what is and will be broken?

a: yes b: no

15: While searching for your spouse, are you willing to live by God's plan for a Christian life?

a: disagree
b: strongly disagree
c: agree
d: strongly agree

What did you learn from this subject?

_____
_____
_____
_____
_____
_____
_____
_____
_____
_____
_____
_____
_____
_____
_____
_____
_____
_____
_____
_____

LOVE

Little word with so much life;

Only you, I don't have to think twice.

Very real feelings about you;

Eve was made for Adam, so what do we do?

The above is to show you, loving you is fun.

I really believe you're the one.

I'm only asking for a commitment

To allow our love to grow!

I'm committed to the time it takes

So let's take it slow.

Committed to say these three words,

I LOVE YOU!

LOVE CAN AND WILL CHANGE PEOPLE!

Hebrew 10-36
For ye have need of patience, that,
after ye have done the will of God,
ye might receive the promise.

Love can and will change people. Love will bring forth growth in one's life. If love can forgive sin; then love can forgive, heal, bless and teach. *So, if love can do these things, why don't we let love grow in our relationship building?* If love could change you to become a better person, would you allow love to be a teacher? Would you change to keep your relationship alive?

Love also gives, but you need to give as well. Can you be a giver in your relationship? Would you care enough to keep your heart warm toward your partner? That's what a giver can give, that is how love can and will change people.

I will only spend a little time here on this subject.

BAD HABITS

If you know you have a bad habit or habits, change them as soon as possible. No one needs to ask you to do this! *This brings forth a giving type of love.* If a companion, asks you to change, realize it may be for the best. But each companion needs to realize change takes time. One may even need to learn how to change. **Remember if you allow love to be a teacher, your relationship will not only grow but become stronger.**

Forgiving is a must in all parts of your companionship. In order to be forgiven, you must forgive.

Forgiving is a part of teaching in your relationship growth. If you can't forgive, sooner or later you are not going to trust. When you don't forgive, you are judging. The Bible is clear on this issue.

(Don't judge lest you be judged).
Matthew 7:1-2 (NKJV)
[1] "Judge not, that you be not judged.
For with what judgment you judge,
you will be judged;
and with the measure you use,
it will be measured back to you.

There may or will be times when we hurt our companion's feelings. This is where he and she must learn to heal and give healing. Saying "I'm sorry" is very hard for many people, especially those who have been hurt in a past relationship. As I have grown, it's not hard for me to say "I'm sorry for my action." You don't need to repeat your wrong actions only grow from your mistakes. This will allow love to grow and become stronger.

Let me ask you to do something. Write out the things in your life that you need to change. We all have things we can change. Is having a loving relationship worth changing for? I believe so, and I'm sure you believe so! So take the time to write out the changes that you should make in your life.

Write out the Bad Habits you have in your life.

_____
_____
_____
_____
_____
_____
_____
_____
_____
_____
_____
_____
_____
_____
_____
_____
_____
_____
_____
_____
_____

I hope you took the time to list a few bad habits that you really need to change in your life.

Now, I would like you to ask God, in the name of Jesus Christ, to help you make these changes.

Please pray about these changes! Remember change take time. Just keep praying.

LOVE CAN AND WILL CHANGE PEOPLE!

1: In Hebrew 10:36, what do you have need for? _____

_____

2: In Hebrew 10:36, after ye have done the will of God, ye might receive what?

_____

_____

3: Love can and will change people. List two things that love has changed in your life. _____

_____

_____

_____

_____

_____

_____

_____

_____

_____

_____

_____

4: Love will bring forth the growth in one's life.

    a: true b: false

5: If love can forgive sin, then love can forgive, heal, bless and teach.

    a: agree
    b: strongly agree
    c: disagree
    d: strongly disagree
    e: I'm not sure

6: If you know you have a bad habit or habits, you should do what in order to change for the better?

    a: acknowledge I have a bad habit
    b: realize it takes time to change
    c: pray and seek God's help
    d: all the above

7: As an adult, if someone brings up that you have a bad habit or an issue that you could change, would you change this habit or issue?

    a: yes b: no

8: The answer you chose for question six, write out why you chose this answer. _____

_____

_____

_____

_____

_____

_____

_____

_____

_____

_____

_____

9: Forgiving is a must in all parts of your companionship. In order to be forgiven you must forgive.

    a: agree
    b: strongly agree
    c: disagree
    d: strongly disagree
    e: I'm not sure

10: If you can't forgive, sooner or later you are not going to trust.

    a: agree
    b: strongly agree
    c: disagree
    d: strongly disagree
    e: I'm not sure

11: When you don't forgive, you are judging.

    a: agree
    b: strongly agree
    c: disagree
    d: strongly disagree
    e: I'm not sure

12: Saying, "I'm sorry" is very hard for many people, especially those who have been hurt in a past relationship.

    a: agree
    b: strongly agree
    c: disagree
    d: strongly disagree
    e: I'm not sure

YOU ARE ON TRIAL FOR LOVE

You have been asked to come to a court of law to prove your love that you have claimed. You're in love with this other person in your relationship. You have to represent yourself, as you read "you are on trial for love."

Take a mental image of this courtroom setting.
The judge happens to be the person you say you love.
The jury is made up of people from your past relationships.

You are walking into the courtroom. Your friends, people from your church and a few of your family members are sitting in this courtroom to give you support. As you walk in, they are looking at you with suspicion. Now, as you walk to your seat, you begin to wonder about yourself and the outcome of this trial. You take your seat, and it's only you and a glass of water that will separate you from the jury and the judge. You are hearing a few comments in the background.

Out walk the people who make up the jury (all of your X's), and they all look at you, one at a time. They are just as dumbfounded as you are. There is a still chill in this courtroom as you wait for the judge to walk out. (By the way the judge didn't know he or she would judge your case, nor did you.) As the judge walks out to take a seat, the judge gives you a smile and wonders what you are going to say. Now, remember, it's up to the jury to make the decision, if you are telling the truth.

The judge reads why you're here, and the judge reads a statement that you must answer. The judge has asked you to prove that you love this person in your relationship. You must convince this jury and the judge. By writing out a detailed outline of facts and reasons why you have a real love for the other person involved. The judge asked that you do this within thirty minutes, and with less than 300 words. Then he hands you pen and paper. Then the judge asks you to begin writing.

Here is where I want you to write out why you love or have loved someone.
You may need more room for this. Use a pad to write on.

Don't look at the next page!
Until you have written out; why you are in love.
If you are not in love at this point in your life, write out why you have been in love before.

The judge has just walked back into the courtroom.

Everyone has taken his or her seat. The judge has given you the allowed time. It is time to hand over the facts and reasons. The judge has asked that you read your statement to the jury and court.

(At this point I want you to go to your mirror and read your statement aloud.)
Just play along I'm trying to get you to understand real love.

You just completed your statement. How do you think the jury and judge took your statement?

Then a man walked into the courtroom. He begins to speak with wisdom, to inform the court and you. He reveals what real love is! The court and you sit back into your seats not knowing what to expect.

There is a sound of thunder as this strange man begins to speak.
"Real relationships need real commitments of love. That you will need to renew everyday of your life. There are three types of love, EROS, PHILIA and AGAPE. I'm here to tell you and this court the truth concerning love. Today, I stand before you with the truth about LOVE!

From the Webster's dictionary:

Eros: It's a Greek word: Sexual love, to love, desire

1: the Greek god of erotic love – *(this could be sexual without real love)*

2: The aggregate of life-preserving instincts that are manifested as impulses to gratify basic needs (as sex), sublimated impulses motivated by the same needs, and impulses serving to protect and preserve the body and mind.

3: often not cap: aspiring and fulfilling love often having a sensual quality: Desire, Yearning

Philia: It's a Greek word: friendship, Dear

1: Tendency toward (someone)

2: Abnormal appetite or liking for (it can also mean (philic: having an affinity for: love (look at the word affinity: 1: kinship, relationship. 2: attractive force: attractive sympathy).

3: Family or brotherly love

Agape: It's a Greek word: love

1: Love feast

2: love – (this is real love)

3: The strongest kind of love

4: God kind of love; unconditional love

Let's look at a few more words out of the dictionary:

Love feast:

1: A meal eaten in common by a Christian congregation in token of brotherly love.

2: A gathering held to promote reconciliation, and good feelings. Or show someone affectionate honor.

Love:

1a: a strong affection for another, arising out of kinship or personal ties

1b: attraction based on sexual desire; affection and tenderness felt by lovers.

1c: affection based on admiration, benevolence, or common interest – an assurance of love.

2: warm attachment, enthusiasm, or devotion.

3: the object of attachment, devotion or admiration.

3b: a beloved person, darling – often used as term of endearment.

4: unselfish loyal and benevolent concern for the good of another.

Love affair:

1: a romantic attachment or episode between lovers.

2: a lively enthusiasm.

Relationship:

1: a romantic or passionate attachment.

Marriage:

1: The institution where men and women are joined in a special kind of social and legal dependence for the purpose of founding and maintaining a family.

1b: the rite by which the married status is affected.

After you had read your statement aloud to the courtroom, how did it match up to what the stranger said? Did the jury and judge accept your statement as the truth? Have you been in any fake relationships? Did you have a real idea of love? Do you have the truth of love now?

Now let's look at these three words (Eros, Philia and Agape) from a Christian point of view.

Eros: It is inspired by the biological structure of human nature (man and woman). The husband and wife, in a good marriage, will love each other romantically and forever! This type of love should be handled in a Christian way (In marriage)! This is not perverted or any type of perversion sexual activities. Sex is something that God cerate for mankind to enjoy and to multiply. It should be performed with care and pleasure and never perversion!

Philia: In a good marriage the husband and wife are also friends. It's a best friend relationship. This type of friendship means companionship, communication and cooperation. (Everyday!) Philia is family love. This is where brotherly love comes from. To be friends.

Agape: Unconditional love, self-giving love, gift of love, the love that goes on loving. Even when love, becomes unlovable. I believe Agape love is not just something that happens to you; it's something you make happen. This is a gift of love. God, Himself, showed this unconditional love. We share this love by faith and by His spirit. Agape love will grow in a real relationship and marriage. That's why we should grow in love, not fall in love!

If people, would take these three words, (Eros, Philia and Agape),
make them into a three cord rope, to make their love stronger,
their love would last a lifetime!

If married companions would only put forth efforts purposely to increase Philia and Agape love, this alone would increase their Eros love. This is when Eros love will flourish if properly nurtured. If people would increase in the area of Eros love, this would reinforce the Philia and Agape love. Now you see why the three strand cord of love will last a lifetime in a marriage! These three types of love will keep and save your companionship!

Love will die when you spend little or no time together, or when you stop sharing activities that are mutually enjoyed! (Remember this!) Love is created or destroyed, if there are or aren't pleasurable activities over a period of time. So stay involved by interacting with each other. Don't let your love die. This is your responsibility! **If couples don't reinforce their love, it will just die.**

Real love requires the ability to put yourself in your companion's place. So you would understand the differences of two very unique personalities. Rather than unfaithfulness, you would have faith, hope and love, the true love of companionship, and the unconditional willingness of each of you (man and woman) to keep your love alive. To understand and resolve these differences through the sharing of your deepest feelings, concerns, attitudes and ideals is a fundamental component of real love, companionship and marriage!

Now, did you know what love is about?
If everyone; could write their statement of love like this.
I believe their love would be a love for a lifetime!

<u>Proverbs 18:22</u>
Whoso findeth a wife findeth a good thing, and obtaineth favor of the LORD.

<u>Hebrews 13:4</u>
Marriage is honourable in all, and the bed undefiled:

Give to another what he or she cannot find anywhere else.
And he or she will keep returning!
One way to do this is to grow into companionship love.

1: What did you learn from this subject?

_____
_____
_____
_____
_____
_____
_____

2: How can you describe the word love now? _____

_____
_____
_____
_____
_____
_____
_____
_____
_____
_____
_____
_____

3: In real life, do you think this is really happening; is your love on trials?

    a: disagree
    b: strongly disagree
    c: agree
    d: strongly agree
    e: I have not thought of this in such a way

4: Does our past bring forth trails in one's life?

    a: disagree
    b: strongly disagree
    c: agree
    d: strongly agree
    e: I have not thought of this in such a way

LIVING TOGETHER VERSUS MARRIAGE

Living together: This is only a temporary ideal; it does not bring forth the companionship of a family unit! I chose to use the word "temporary" to describe those who choose to live together. I did this for a few reasons.

1: Living together has no real foundation of commitment. This type of commitment is day by day and may last a few years at the most. Not a lifetime.

2: There is no oneness in living together; the two people will live under established rules. There is no unity in their companionship, just titles and union.

3: More than likely one of the two will be used as a "hang around person."

4: There is no home; it's just a house.

5: What is yours is yours, and what is theirs is theirs. Everything is singled out, without any unity.

6: For most, love doesn't grow into marriage or companionship. One may be happy with this type of relationship. If love doesn't keep growing, it just dies! This is what happens when we live together.

7: Living together is just temporary. There is no commitment for a lifetime of companionship!

8: The relationship love may never grow into companionship love.

9: When God gave the gift of marriage, he took two people and made them one in unity. This cannot happen when you choose to live together; it is just a union!

10: There is a real difference in companionship love in marriage versus the love that's in a live -together life style!

Here are a few statements, made by people who live together.

* <u>Why buy the milk when it's free</u>? *What I have said to that statement is, "Love that is real will grow toward marriage. For marriage was given as a free gift from God Himself!"*

* <u>We are living together to see if it will work.</u> *So where is the real commitment? I say; work toward marriage and allow your love and commitment to grow and stay alive! That is worth working for. You are blessed when you enter marriage.*

* <u>I have fear of marriage.</u> *What you are really saying is,; "I'm not committed to marriage," or "I don't have the knowledge of a real companionship relation."*

- <u>We haven't made a pre-marriage agreement.</u> *I say to you "Get an attorney that can help you!"*

- <u>It will not work.</u> *I say, "it takes a lot of work, and you have no commitment!"*

- <u>It's cheaper to live together than to live single.</u> *This is a true statement. That's why God said two is better than one. Marriage is God's plan! A man needs a woman, as much as a woman needs a man. Companionship in marriage can and will save the two of you a lot of money and time.*

- <u>I just want someone to be here or a "hang around person".</u> *This is one of the greatest mistakes we see with live-in couples. You may be living with someone until he or she gets over his or her issues like debt, loneliness, depression, sexual lifestyle, change in life, renovation of house and so on. My question to you is, "Are you being used?"*

- <u>If someone doesn't believe in marriage there may be a few reasons for this.</u> Like he or she really doesn't love you, just has you in their life until they think he or she have met someone else that he or she thinks is better, doesn't understand love or can't love; he or she doesn't want to answer to a relationship lifestyle, and so on.

List some of your reasons why you don't believe in Marriage.

_____

_____

_____

_____

_____

_____

_____

_____

_____

_____

_____

_____

_____

_____

_____

_____

_____

_____

_____

_____

1: Which is better, marriage or living together? The answer is in your heart.

    a: marriage b: living together

2: Write out why you think living together is acceptable_____

_____

_____

_____

_____

_____

_____

_____

_____

_____

_____

_____

_____

_____

_____

_____

_____

_____

_____

_____

_____

3: Write out why you think marriage is acceptable: _____

_____

_____

_____

_____

_____

_____

_____

_____

_____

_____

_____

_____

_____

_____

_____

FRIENDSHIP OR LOVE

Use this as an open discussion session. Spend some time talking about this subject!

Friendship comes from the word Friend. What is a friend?

1: one attached to another by respect or affection.

2: acquaintance

3: one who is not hostile.

4: one who supports or favors something.

5: a member of a society of friends

Don't mistake friendship,
For someone who isn't worth having a long term relationship with!
Wisdom is needed here!

Love: What is love?

1: strong affection.

2: warm attachment.

3: attraction based on Godly sexual desires (to be married).

4: a real beloved person

5: unselfish, loyal and concerned for others.

Love is worth a real and lifelong commitment.
True love is hard to find and must be kept alive.
By your commitments, everyday!
I want to show you a true commitment, spoken by a woman.
If Ruth can speak this way from her heart,
Why can't man and woman.
Understand the power of commitment through real love and compassion?

Ruth 1:16,17 *And Ruth said, Entreat me not to leave thee, or to return from following after thee: for whither thou goest, I will go; and where thou lodgest, I will lodge: thy people shall be my people, and thy God my God: Where thou diest, I will die, and there will I be buried: the LORD do so to me, and more also, if ought but death part thee and me.*

CHANGING FOR A BETTER RELATIONSHIP

A great relationship is worth any and all changes that come from either companion. To have a real loving and caring relationship you must grow. To grow means to change. Change is needed in a real loving and caring relationship. Companions shouldn't have to be asked to change. Again change takes time. If your partner points out something, take notice of what he or she said. It does take a lot of effort to change. *I agree that one must be able to change himself or herself.* **Let your companion change themself.** This will make the relationship stronger.

If you are not willing to change, why have a relationship? Time is a real factor when it comes to new changes. Two people (companions) must realize that they will have real differences. This is true about all relationships. This rule applies to all new companions. ***Your relationship is worth all the work it takes to keep a relationship alive.***

Work through your differences,
then watch love grow
To last a lifetime!

Changing for a greater relationship starts with you!
If you are dating someone who lives by this next statement,
"It's my way or the high way!"! Get rid of them!

You don't want someone who isn't willing to change to make the relationship greater! You don't need a relationship with someone who talks foolishly. Don't waste your time! When a person will not change for the better of a relationship, just move on and find a greater person! Believe me, there are single adults looking to find a loving companion!

Remember that change is not about what's right or wrong.
It's about creating a great team and companionship!
It's also about you as a teammate and a companion!

REWARDS IN ONE'S LIFE ARE DETERMINED
BY THE PROBLEMS HE OR SHE SOLVES

Proverbs 1:5

A wise man (or woman) will hear, and will increase learning;
and a man (or woman) of understanding
shall attain unto wise counsels.

What areas do you think you have to change? _____

_____

_____

_____

_____

_____

_____

_____

_____

_____

_____

_____

1: Do you believe you will have to change in order to have a better relationship?

    a: disagree
    b: strongly disagree
    c: agree
    d: strongly agree

2: A great relationship is worth any and all change.

    a: disagree
    b: strongly disagree
    c: agree
    d: strongly agree

3: To grow we must change both mentally and spiritually. Does this involve God's plan for you?

    a: disagree
    b: strongly disagree
    c: agree
    d: strongly agree

4: If love can change a person, we should allow our companion to change himself or herself?

    a: disagree
    b: strongly disagree
    c: agree
    d: strongly agree

5: How much time is required to change someone's bad habits or issues?

    a: that depends on what it is
    b: that depends on the level of addiction
    c: depends on one's motivation level
    d: all the above

6: If you are not willing to change for the better of a relationship, should you involve someone in a relationship?

    a: yes b: no

7: Concerning your answer to question six, why did you choose yes or no?

_____

_____

_____

_____

_____

_____

_____

_____

_____

_____

_____

8: Two people (companions) must realize that they will have real differences. This is true about all relationships.

    a: true b: false

9: Is your relationship worth all the work it takes to keep a relationship alive?

    a: disagree
    b: strongly disagree
    c: agree
    d: strongly agree

10: In your own words, what do you think about Proverbs 1:5?_____

_____

_____

_____

_____

_____

YOUR NOTES:_____

IMAGINATION RELATIONSHIPS

Don't allow yourself to be a part of this deceiving relationship. If you are living in an imagination life style, that's a bad habit! A person that's in an ***imaginary relationship*** will fall in love, versus grow in love. He or she just imagines love in a relationship, and this is a false love! As you grow toward love and a relationship; you must change your bad habits.

Here is an example of an Imagination / Relationship

Two people meet. They go out. Then they touch, kiss or have sex. (Sex is not love.) After this point, one of them will say; "I'm in love", they will do this within a few days to less than 14 days. This is far from the truth! **It takes time to trust someone. Without trust how can you love?** *He or she has only allowed their imagination to take over his or her emotions. They are not in control of their reality! He or she may not even know this.* **This is why I give great caution about people who fall in love quickly**. *Stay away from this type of relationship. He or she will only say they love you. Until their imagination tells them that he or she loves someone else.* **This is one of many types of false relationships! Just because someone said they love you, does not mean they really do. Love is a word that is often misused! Ask that person who said he or she loves you, why and how he or she loves you. If they say "I don't know; I just love you," this is not love! This is a warning given to those who seek a long term relationship that will lead to marriage!**

One must build trust in order to love.
If your trust doesn't grow, where is the love?
Don't allow yourself to be pulled into a false relationship.
How can we avoid this?

Ask the person you're trying to date or court, about his or her wants in a relationship. **Open that person's mind and look at their imagination and reality.** When he or she speaks about issues of control, domination, ruling, fear, consuming your time, and how much attention he or she really needs or wants, be very cautious here. If they have pointed out these issues without reality of a real relationship, it may be best to avoid this relationship.

People in a real relationship will build goals together! This is a working relationship!

I'm here to tell you that a great relationship comes with a lot of quality work and time.

You can count on this! Time is part of a relationship's foundation!In a fake relationship, a person will try to place a title on you quickly.Remember you are not a title!

1 Corinthians 10:13
There hath no temptation taken you but such as is common to man (woman): but God is faithful, who will not suffer you to be tempted above that ye are able; but will with the temptation also make a way to escape, that ye may be able to bear it.
This one verse will protect you, all the days of your life.
So what does one do to keep them self out of an Imaginary Relationship?

1: Ask them about their dream relationship?

2: Ask them how many relationship or marriages they have been in?

3: Ask them why they got a divorce, and about each time they got divorced?

4: Ask them about all past relationships; see if they will give details?

5: Ask them how many people they had sex with in the past few years?

6: Ask them if they set goals in relationships? What kind of goals do they have?

7: Ask them what type of person are they looking for?

8: Ask them if they are looking for a long term relationship?

9: How do they treat their family members and friends?

10: Then ask yourself is this the person for me?

You owe it to yourself to ask these ten questions. When you ask these ten questions, go back at a later date and repeat these questions. See if they change their story, find out why. Get as much information about someone before you grow in love.

The truth is in the eyes. Please remember this!
Don't become a part of an imaginary relationship.
They will only drag you down.
So beware!

<u>James 1:12</u>

Blessed is the man (or woman) that endureth temptation:
for when he is tried,
he (or she) shall receive the crown of life,
which the Lord hath promised to them that love him.

What you are willing to walk away from.
Will determine what God will bring into your life!

1: Don't allow yourself to be a part of a deceiving relationship.

    a: disagree
    b: strongly disagree
    c: agree
    d: strongly agree

2: It takes time to trust someone. Without trust, how can you love? Do you believe you should trust someone before you love that person?

    a: disagree
    b: strongly disagree
    c: agree
    d: strongly agree

3: Concerning question three, in your own words, why did you choose the answer you did?

_____

_____

_____

_____

_____

_____

_____

_____

_____

_____

_____

_____

4: What should you use great caution in?

    a: allowing two weeks to pass before you fall in love
    b: place love before trust
    c: He or she fell in love with me
    d: all the above

5: Just because someone can say he or she love you, does he or she really love you?

    a: It's true he or she love me
    b: Time will tell if he or she love me
    c: I would ask how he or she loves me
    d: Has there been enough time and trust for him or her to say, "I love you".

6: Concerning question three, in your own words why did you choose the answer you did?

_____

_____

_____

_____

_____

_____

_____

_____

_____

_____

_____

_____

7: If someone said he or she loved you but do not know why, is this a warning?

    a: true b: false

8: How can you avoid a false relationship?

    a: Come to know a person over time
    b: Build a trusting relationship
    c: Do not allow someone to fall in love
    d: All the above

9: In your own words, write out some ways to keep yourself from entering a false relationship.

_____

_____

_____

_____

_____

_____

_____

EXPECTATION / IMATINATION

Expectation

In this area of our behavior, we can cause ourselves a lot of problems. Within our **expectation,** there is anticipation of something happening; a confident belief or strong hope that a particular event will happen. When we have a notion of something, as a mental image of something expected, we often compare this to reality.

With our *expectation* comes truth; we must learn to control this expectation behavior. Our **anticipation** of our **expectation** can and will cause us to be misdirected. *When we have hope or high hope in something that may or may not happen, we become disappointment.*

This is when **expectation** will cause you to have a problem with your mental state. **Confusion starts here.** When you allow hope to be a false hope, you are not in control of your mind. If we do not learn to control our expectations early in life; we will have a hard time with this as adults. We can grow to expect too much out of people, friends, family members and love ones. This is often done without understanding all of the information of truth. **Relationships can be and have been destroyed over one's expectation!**

Your foundation of life should never be built on Expectation!
Either you are in control of your mind
or
your mind is in control of you!

Imagination

Imagination is where we have the ability to visualize; and to form images and ideas in the mind, especially things we have never seen or experienced. **One's imagination can be both good and bad, for it is the creative part of one's mind.** This is the part of the mind where ideals, thoughts, and images are formed. This is one area of the mind where we can have created resources, like the ways to deal with difficult problems. In this area, we can resolve problems or repair things. **But this area of imagination must be developed.** We can also be creative with our imagination. One's imagination must be used in a controlled way.

We can allow our imagination to take over. When this happens we can have fear and wrong creative images that are not in the reality of life, wrong ideas, and thoughts. Sin can be found in imagination. One's imagination can lead to depression. If you don't control your imagination who will? Here is where people end up with more than one personality. This is where satan / the devil can control you! An out of control imagination can be deadly!

Yes, imagination can be a great and good thing as well. Great things have been created out of one's imagination. Art, music, and writing come from our imagination. When one is in control of his or her mind; imagination is a good thing. This is when imagination helps develop people.

Children have their parents to help instruct their use of imaginations. This is a part of childhood. But we as adults have been influenced by outside sources; that are not role models of a good life such as, movies, bad characters, association with occults, music with bad lyrics, drugs and alcohol, unhealthy practices of eating that keeps our pH level in the acidic state, and depression. This area of life and behaviors will cause you to sin and will take you down a road of to Hell. It has been said so many times; that sin starts with our imagination. When we get committed to a thought of imagination, is it for the good or bad? You must ask yourself this each time you enter your imagination. We are not born to be a bad person, we are taught to be bad people. We are born in hope of having good values that gives us the gifts of understanding.

We must watch over our association with people and influences.
Acts 24:16 And here do I exercise myself, to have always a conscience void of offence toward God, and toward men (mankind).

1: Expectation: a confident belief or strong hope that a particular event will happen, a mental image of something expected, often compared to its reality.

    a: disagree
    b: strongly disagree
    c: agree
    d: strongly agree

2: Concerning question one, in your own words, why did you choose the answer you did?

_____

_____

_____

_____

_____

_____

_____

_____

3: Imagination: the ability to form images and ideas in the mind, especially of things never seen or experienced directly, the part of the mind where ideas, thoughts, and images are formed.

    a: disagree
    b: strongly disagree
    c: agree
    d: strongly agree

4: Concerning question three, in your own words, why did you choose the answer you did?

_____

_____

_____

_____

_____

_____

_____

_____

_____

_____

_____

5: Can sin be found in our imagination?

    a: disagree
    b: strongly disagree
    c: agree
    d: strongly agree

6: Here is where people end up with more than one personality. This is where Satan / the Devil can control person! An out of control imagination can be deadly!

    a: disagree
    b: strongly disagree
    c: agree
    d: strongly agree

7: Children have their parents to help instruct their use of their imaginations. This is a part of childhood. But we as adults have been influenced by outside sources that are not role models of a good life.

    a: true b: false

OUR EXPECTATIONS OF PEOPLE

In this part of our thinking, we get ourselves into trouble with our imagination, disappointments, anger and lack of wisdom. *Let's say you meet someone who you want to spend time with. You may have already set your expectation level of what this person or this relationship could be. This is where you will become disappointed. This will also cause you to stop growing in your relationship.* That's like saying, "I fell in love with a one-sided vision!" **When people set their expectations from the beginning or too early in the relationships, they are setting up their relationships for failure.** As love grows, so does the relationship. *We must learn to allow the relationship to grow before we have any expectation!*

Before you have any expectation, allow yourself some time, to just have fun as you come to know the other person. Companionship comes with time. You must become friends first in all relationships. You must get past the attraction as well. You should allow love to start to grow, (like in three months or so)! Then talk together about the real expectation of a relationship as companions. This will allow your love to grow on the foundation of companionship.

Write out some of your mistakes that you made with your expectation.

_____
_____
_____
_____
_____
_____
_____
_____
_____
_____
_____
_____
_____
_____
_____

**As love grows,
so does the
Relationship**

DON'T MESS UP SOMEONE'S LIFE

I want to hit the nail really hard here!
You and I don't have the right to mess up someone's life!

If you are using someone to fill-in your time because of your loneliness and desires, this is not of God at all. Always remember when you hurt someone that he or she is a child of God. (This will be returned to you and your kind sooner or later, but it will happen in God's time). This is something I have done: Each time I meet someone with whom I had sex with or a bad relationship, I have asked her to forgive me for my action and fault. For the most part she is shocked and willing to forgive me. I then explained to her that I'm living for God, Jesus, and The Holy Spirit. **When we have sex outside of marriage, someone is set up to get hurt.** That's a fact that you and everyone else can take to the bank! Why are 40 to 50 percent of adults single today in America?

1: No commitment.

2: No faith or real love

3: Don't give a care

4: Rejection

5: I can make it on my own

6: I can go out with whomever I want

7: No fear

8: No knowledge of a family life

9: Doesn't live like Christ

10: Any other reason you can think of

(This is just a small list, what's yours?)

These are just a few facts I am sure you and I can come up with a list as long as my arm!

But the real reason there is no commitment among the single adults. They can't love, or they are afraid to love! Why do single adults mislead one another to the point where someone is really hurt? *All the free sex you had in a relationship will not cover the pain or hurt that comes after a false relationship! To the one that is using or* *misleading someone else, believe me when I say this: YOUR DAY IS COMING, AND IT'S WITHIN A SHORT DISTANCE OF GOD'S HANDS!* Then where will you stand?

What about those who think having sex is love? You are foolish, and you don't know what love is truly about! Your day is coming. Believe me! What goes around comes around! Do not hang around people who are foolish!

Running from one relationship to another; most people are always looking for green grass. This will only cause you to fall. Anything that is hot can burn you!

Proverbs 14:14 *The backslider in heart shall be filled with his own ways....*

Jeremiah 15:6 *Thou hast forsaken me, saith the LORD, thou art gone backward; therefore I will stretch out my hand against thee, and destroy thee; I am weary with repenting.*

Proverbs 17:20 *He that hath a forward heart findeth no good: and he that hath a perverse tongue falleth into mischief.*

Psalm 119:11 *Thy word have I hid in mine heart, that I might not sin against thee.*

James 4:7 *Submit yourselves therefore to God. Resist the devil, and he will flee from you.*

Something to watch out for. Take a real warning here: People can be addicted to other people. What am I saying here? There are types of single adults who must have someone else in their life. They are a hang-around person. They are misleading, and can or will cause you to have or be in a false relationship. They will use you until they find something they think is better. They will often take advantage of you sexually, and financially have you work on their homes or cars, or use you to show you off to family members, their friend or co-workers. Just to say they're having a relationship. They will also do this to attract someone new!

1: Do you have the right to mess up someone's life in a false relationship?

    yes or no

2: Concerning question one, why did you choose the answer you did? _____

_____

_____

_____

_____

_____

_____

_____

_____

3: Always remember when you hurt someone, that he or she is a child of God. (This will be returned to you and your kind sooner or later, but it will happen in God's time.)

    a: disagree
    b: strongly disagree
    c: agree
    d: strongly agree

4: This is something I have done: Each time I meet someone with whom I had sex with or a bad relationship, I have asked her to forgive me for my action and fault. If you knew you misled someone into a false relationship, and now you understand you hurt them in this false relationship, and you met him or her again, what would you choose to do?

    a: explain to him or her I was wrong for my action
    b: admit that you need to apologize
    c: it is best to forget this happened
    d: I do not feel the need to apologize

5: There are two ways to have sin in one's life. There are sins, that are against God and sins, against mankind. If you have sinned against God or mankind, what should you do if you are a Christian? In your own words, write a small response to this question.

_____
_____
_____
_____
_____
_____
_____
_____
_____
_____
_____
_____

6: Did you know you could sin against God or mankind?

    a: yes b: no

7: When we have sex outside of marriage, someone is set up to get hurt.

    a: disagree
    b: strongly disagree
    c: agree
    d: strongly agree

8: Concerning question seven, explain your answer:

_____
_____
_____
_____
_____
_____
_____
_____
_____
_____
_____

9: What about those who think, having sex is love? Have you ever done this or felt this way?

    a: yes b: no

10: Running from one relationship to another; most people are always looking for green grass. This will only cause you to fall. Anything that is hot can burn you!

    a: true b: false

BAD HABITS

Your bad habits have not taken you anywhere! *James 5:16 Confess your faults one to another, and pray one for another, that ye may be healed. The effectual fervent prayer of a righteous man availeth much.* **1 John 1:9** *If we confess our sins, He (God or Jesus) is faithful and just to forgive us our sins, and to cleanse us from all unrighteousness.*

2 Timothy 2:16 *But shun profane and vain babblings; for they will increase unto more ungodliness.*

Let me suggest that you read the book of Proverbs! Of all the books of the Bible, this book will open the door to a better life. A book of Kings and leadership, the book of Proverbs is a book of understanding, leadership, correction, discipline and respect. I used to read this book three to four times a year, when I was a young Christian. This is a great book to bring forth a change in your character. When you finish studying this book, study the book of Proverbs. **If you really want to change your life, you will need a lot of discipline!**

Find someone you can trust to confess your faults to. You should be transparent with only one or two people *(warning: I can keep a secret, but it's the people I tell who can't)*. This is why you should confess your faults with only a few or just one person. **I BELIEVE THAT MEN SHOULD DEAL WITH MEN, AND WOMEN SHOULD DEAL WITH WOMEN!** Why should we confess? The Bible tells us to. By doing this, you are asking to repent and to be forgiven for your faults, sins, and your bad habits. *You are in charge of your mind; it is up to you to do what is right in the eyes of God.* You know what is wrong, you know what is right; this is because of the spirit God gave you at creation! It all starts with respecting yourself and other people. Guard your tongue, and weigh out your thoughts and opinions before you speak! ***I assure you, if you cannot control your tongue, you are not in control of your mind either!*** **Our tongue is the most horrific habit we will have to break! When you start controlling your tongue, you will start controlling your mind. *What comes out of a person's mouth, will characterize him or her.*** People who are foolish cannot control their mouths! The Bible cautions us about being a fool! Bad habits can lead to a sinful personality!

What could you do to improve your character? You cannot change your character without love. You will have to love yourself first without arrogance or pride. Being arrogant or being prideful will keep you from God and being spiritual as a Christian.

Everything takes time, and so does changing your bad habits.

1ˢᵗ, start controlling your tongue.

2ⁿᵈ, be accountable in all you do. You need to be responsible for all that you do!

3ʳᵈ, you may need to improve on your appearance; your appearance does put forth an attitude. If you allow pride to direct your appearance; who are you? It does not hurt to clean up one's appearance.

4ᵗʰ, learn to forgive everyone.

5ᵗʰ, don't judge.

6ᵗʰ, don't gossip.

7ᵗʰ, learn to be a real Christian.

1: **James 5:16** Confess your faults one to another, and pray one for another, that ye may be healed. The effectual fervent prayer of a righteous man availeth much. (How does this verse apply to you and how would you use this verse?)

_____
_____
_____
_____
_____
_____
_____
_____
_____
_____

2: **1 John 1:9** If we confess our sins, He (God or Jesus) is faith, and just to forgive us our sins, and to cleanse us from all unrighteousness. (My question to you is should you confess your sins and how would this help you as a Christian)?

_____
_____
_____
_____
_____
_____
_____
_____
_____

3: Can you apply James 5:16 and 1 John 1:9 to your life now that you know these two verses?

    a: disagree
    b: strongly disagree
    c: agree
    d: strongly agree

4: The book of Proverbs is a book of wisdom, understanding, leadership, correction, discipline and respect.

    a: disagree
    b: strongly disagree
    c: agree
    d: strongly agree
    e: I never read or studied the book of Proverbs

5: If you really want to change your life, you will need a lot of discipline!

    a: true b: false

6: Find someone you can trust to confess your faults with; you should be transparent with only one or two people (only a few); *(warning: I can keep a secret, but it's the people I tell secrets to who can't)*.

    a: disagree
    b: strongly disagree
    c: agree
    d: strongly agree

7: Unless they are a pastor or on a ministry team, I believe that men should deal with men, and women should deal with women when it comes to confessions?

    a: disagree
    b: strongly disagree
    c: agree
    d: strongly agree

8: List some ways to change your bad habits:_____

_____

_____

_____

_____

_____

_____

_____

_____

BE AWARE OF ONE'S BODY LANGUAGE

Body language: the gestures and mannerisms by which a person communicates with his or her body. Body language can show signs of behavioral problems. Body language can also show signs of quality behaviors.

Communication skills and Body language = People skills

I just want to make you aware of body language. It is part of the makeup of a person. Body language will allow you to see a person for who he or she really is. *When body language goes along with one's communication skills at the beginning, you are looking at a person who is being oneself. And if one's body language is different from one's communication skill, there is a reason for this.* Remember, you must take time to know someone. *People will use their body language first before they use their communication skills.* **When a quality person has good body gestures, it shows. When a person has aggression in his or her body language, this will give you the first sign of trouble.** Body language will happen before poor communication skills. Everyone can speak nice, but most people don't control their body language.

Signs to look for when someone has aggression: Hitting things, pointing fingers, holding up their hands a lot, faking hitting things, (including people), kicking things, fake kicking, grabbing, biting his or her lip, tongue, fingers, and so on. These are just a few signs. *Most people who have body language aggression have real habits, of using their gestures. Habits can be a warning.*

Signs to look for when someone has quality behaviors: hugs, handshakes, looks at you when he or she talks with happiness, waves, smiles, makes signs of peace, looks like he or she is listening. These are just a few things.

There is a lot to say about this subject. You really have to come to know someone, in order to understand one's body language. That's another reason to take your time in a relationship. *It may take 30 to 60 days for a person to act normally. But in time, you will see his or her body language.*

1: Body language can show signs of behavioral problems. Body language can also show signs of quality behaviors.

    a: disagree
    b: strongly disagree
    c: agree
    d: strongly agree

2: When a quality person has good body gestures, it shows. When a person has aggression in his or her body language, this will give you the first sign of trouble.

    a: true b: false

3: Body language will happen before poor communications skills. Everyone can speak nicely. But most people don't control their body language.

    a: disagree
    b: strongly disagree
    c: agree
    d: strongly agree

4: Signs to look for when someone has aggression in his or her body language; write these out in your own words: _____

_____
_____
_____
_____
_____
_____
_____
_____
_____
_____

5: Signs to look for when someone has quality behaviors in his or her body language; write these out in your own words:_____

_____
_____
_____
_____
_____
_____
_____
_____
_____

6: Write out some of your body language that you use when you are having quality body language:

_____
_____
_____
_____
_____
_____
_____
_____
_____
_____
_____
_____
_____
_____

7: Write out some of your body language that you use when you are upset: _____

_____
_____
_____
_____
_____
_____
_____
_____
_____
_____
_____
_____

8: Write out some of your body language that you use when you are being aggressive:

_____
_____
_____
_____
_____
_____
_____
_____
_____
_____
_____
_____
_____

9: Write out some of the body language that you use to get someone's attention:

_____
_____
_____
_____
_____
_____
_____
_____
_____
_____
_____
_____
_____

10: Note any other body language: _____
_____
_____
_____
_____
_____
_____
_____
_____
_____
_____

Notes: _____
_____
_____
_____
_____
_____
_____
_____
_____
_____
_____
_____
_____
_____
_____
_____
_____
_____

SIGNS TO LOOK FOR BEFORE YOU ENTER INTO ANOTHER BAD RELATIONSHIP

1: He or she wants sex fast: *They do this for many reasons: they may be hurt; it's their way of life, to get back at someone else and to feel a need to be with someone all night. They use you as a fill in. They may not be able to be alone. They hurt and feel the need to have someone for a time, so that they aren't alone. Sex to them may be a way to say, "I love you", or let them think they love you.*

2: Wants you to meet his or her family as soon as possible: *Just to show off what he or she has found in another relationship. Look at what I got! He or she may do this to let the person that hurt him or her see that he or she can get someone else. He or she may do this to get back into a past relationship!*

3: A taker: *You may find yourself buying things for him or her. A good person would tell you, "You don't have to do this. I don't feel good about taking the things you are giving me".* **The taker will just keep taking until he or she finds someone else or greener grass so to speak.** *Your gift may not mean anything to the taker. Your gift doesn't make love real in the taker's life. He or she only uses people. A taker is a thief and a liar! He or she will stay with you until he or she finds greener grass.*

4: When someone is not trying to lead or make the relationship grow: *He or she is just using you to have fun. They are called fake lovers, and this will cause someone to get really hurt. They are having sex to fill their desires.*

5: You are the one who creates the things to do: *The other person doesn't try to have activities from his or her part of the relationship. He or she is just there to enjoy himself or herself and use you. He or she will do this until they find greener grass! Look out for this type!*

6: Agrees to everything you want to do or what you say: *He or she does this to have something to fall back on, so he or she can say, "I'm tired of doing it your way". This is the scapegoat, and he or she was just there for a free ride!*

7: His or her whole family may be in sin: *This creates a bad past for him or her to overcome. He or she may be living for only himself or herself. This may not always be true, but for the most part, it is! He or she will drag you down into their Hell!*

8: Someone who can't make decisions: *This is a person who has no motivation in a relationship. Once again he or she is there just to have someone near him or her just for fun.*

This type of adult is likely to spend time to use someone else, again as a fill in type of relationship.

Beware of this! People who don't know are people who can cause the most Hell!

9: May want you to do things for him or her: *Like, fixing things in his or her house, share in expense, pay his or her bills, doing his or her laundry; he or she always has something for you to do. Remember, a relationship isn't being a slave!*

<u>**Proverbs 27:6**</u> **Faithful are the wounds of a friend; but the kisses of an enemy are deceitful.**

<u>**Proverbs 17:17**</u> **A friend loveth at all times....**

<u>**Leviticus 19:11**</u> **Ye shall not steal, neither deal falsely, neither lie one to another.**

I want you to write out a list of other signs to look for before you enter into another bad relationship. Discuss this with your friends, as well.

_____

_____

_____

_____

_____

_____

_____

_____

_____

_____

_____

_____

_____

_____

_____

_____

_____

_____

_____

_____

_____

_____

SO INVOLVED, YOU DON'T SEE THE TRUTH

It all starts with finding someone with whom you have chosen to go out with. The first few dates are okay to great. Maybe you and the other person become attracted to each other. Now that these new feelings are fitting together, the two of you become more involved. You start doing the little things for each other. You two are doing these things because it makes you feel good. This is where you become *so involved you don't see the truth*. When you do these little things and then they turn into bigger things. The little things make you feel good, and the bigger things will make you feel great. During this time, you're not putting a check on the real issue such as truth. I don't want you to be suspicious of everyone you date, but I do want you to be aware. **You don't want to put your heart in front of the truth.** You must trust before you grow in love. **Build a relationship based on truth not feelings!**

When you are in the first stages of a relationship, take your time. Good feelings can be one-sided. See if the other person can make you feel good. Allow a relationship to grow before you start loving. One must hold on to his or her heart, to know the truth.

Trust should come before love!

Proverbs 3:5-6
Trust in the LORD with all thine heart;
And lean not unto thine own understanding.
In all thy ways acknowledge Him (the LORD),
And He (the LORD) shall direct thy paths.

Matthew 26: 41
Watch and pray, that ye enter not into temptation:
The spirit indeed is willing,
but the flesh is weak.

1: So involved, you don't see the truth. Do you believe this could happen to someone?

   a: disagree
   b: strongly disagree
   c: agree
   d: strongly agree

2: Concerning question one, why did you choose your answer?

_____
_____
_____
_____
_____
_____
_____
_____
_____
_____
_____
_____

3: You don't want to put your heart in front of the truth. You must trust before you grow in love. Build a trust based on truth, not feelings!

    a: disagree
    b: strongly disagree
    c: agree
    d: strongly agree

4: Concerning question three; why did you choose your answer?

_____
_____
_____
_____
_____
_____
_____
_____
_____
_____
_____

5: When you are in the first stages of a relationship, take your time.

    a: true b: false

6: One must hold on to his or her heart, to know the truth.

    a: disagree
    b: strongly disagree
    c: agree
    d: strongly agree

7: Concerning question six; why did you choose your answer?

_____
_____
_____
_____
_____
_____
_____
_____
_____
_____
_____
_____

CONTROLLING YOUR TONGUE

Proverbs 8:13
The fear of the Lord is to hate evil:
pride, and arrogance, and the evil way,
and the forward mouth, do I (GOD) hate.

Arrogant: offensively exaggerating one's own importance.

God hates a forward tongue. What more can be written on this subject? But yet, we do it every day. Somewhere, someday, somehow, we all need to learn to control our tongue. Controlling ones' tongue is something we learn and have to practice. This generation of people has lost touch with this issue. But I will assure you if you don't control your tongue, life for you will be tough. The Bible makes it real clear, to safeguard your tongue.

You know as well as I do, that we must have great speaking skills in all relationships. When you speak with an evil tongue, you are condemning yourself! When you are not speaking with kindness you are dismantling the foundation of your relationship.

If you know you are harming a relationship by not controlling your tongue, why would someone have to ask you to stop speaking in a way that you know offends people?

A word of warning! Don't fall in love with someone who cannot control their own tongue. *Most people, who are not in control of their tongue, may not be fully in control of their mind either!* These types of people often speak without reason, they just make noise! Don't get mixed up with someone like this!

Proverbs 10:11
The mouth of a righteous man (or woman) is a well of life:
But violence covereth the mouth of the wicked.
(Read chapter six of Proverbs.)
Proverbs 6:16,19
These six things doth the Lord hate: yea, seven are an abomination unto him (the Lord)
A false witness that speaketh lies, and he that soweth discord among brethren (or loved ones).

*I want to invite you to read **James 3:1-12**, to get a full understanding of this passage!*

1: Should we learn to control our tongue?

    a: yes b: no

2: Arrogant: offensively exaggerating one's own importance.

    a: disagree
    b: strongly disagree
    c: agree
    d: strongly agree

3: Why do you think God hates a forward tongue? _____

_____

_____

_____

_____

_____

_____

4: We must have great speaking skills in all relationships.

    a: disagree
    b: strongly disagree
    c: agree
    d: strongly agree

5: When you are not speaking with kindness, you are dismantling the foundation of your relationship.

    a: disagree
    b: strongly disagree
    c: agree
    d: strongly agree

6: Don't fall in love with someone, who cannot control with his or her own tongue.

    a: disagree
    b: strongly disagree
    c: agree
    d: strongly agree

7: Most people, who cannot control their tongues, may not be fully in control of their mind either!

    a: disagree
    b: strongly disagree
    c: agree
    d: strongly agree

EASILY OFFENDED

Proverbs 11:14
Where no counsel is, the people fall:
But in the multitude of counselors
There is safety.

Let's look at the word "offend" to see its roots.

Offend: *sin, transgress, to cause discomfort or pain, hurt, to cause dislike or vexation, annoy.*

It's in these areas that you get offended. You can get offended because of a bad day. You can get offended by a misunderstanding. The way you speak can offend. Our level of people skills can offend. The way you handle your differences can cause a person to become offended. The way you treat people can cause someone to be offended. ***The willingness to change the mistakes one makes will not offend someone.*** I can write pages on how we get offended, **but I want you to think about all the ways you offend people.** When you know you are offending someone, you should stop this action. If you make a mistake, admit it. When you offend someone accidentally, without intent or through carelessness, give him or her time to understand what caused this discomfort. You don't always need to say, I'm sorry. But it's a great thing to say, "I'm sorry, and I care enough to say this!"

Remember, you cannot change the truth!
If you offend someone, address it but be nicely detailed.
If someone offends you, address it but be nicely detailed.
The truth does two things.
It will inform and change people, if you allow it to.
The truth will set you free.

So, I'm asking you to stop offending people.
Never call someone a name, or degrade anyone.
When we really love one another,
We should never offend anyone we love!
There shouldn't be any transgressions in a real relationship.
You have to trust and have peace to love someone!

1: Proverbs 11:14 (Please fill in these blanks) Where (*there is*) no _____
   the_____fall: But in the multitude of _____
   there is safety.

2: What does the word "offend" mean to you?_____
   _____
   _____
   _____
   _____
   _____

3: What offends you? _____
   _____
   _____
   _____
   _____
   _____

4: The willingness to change the mistakes one makes will not offend someone else.

   a: disagree
   b: strongly disagree
   c: agree
   d: strongly agree

5: I want you to think about and write out the ways you offend people.

   _____
   _____
   _____
   _____
   _____
   _____

6: When we know we are offending someone, should we stop this action?

   a: disagree
   b: strongly disagree
   c: agree
   d: strongly agree

7: We don't always need to say, "I'm sorry". But it's a great thing to say, "I'm sorry,
   and I care enough to say this!"

   a: disagree
   b: strongly disagree
   c: agree
   d: strongly agree

DEALING WITH YOUR ANGER

You will have to deal with your anger. Don't let this grow at all in you! *Let me ask you this, what is to blame when you have issues? It is the issue, which must be fixed, changed, and understood! This may be hard for you to accept, but it's true.* In all relationships the last thing you need, is anger in the relationship. If you know you need to change; just change. This is a lot easier than anger and destroying your relationship. Anger can ruin your health and it can kill you. Anger will cause you to sin and cause you great pain. Anger only hurts! Just forgive and rebuild your life. Anger will only bring you to a lower level of life. Anger will keep you hurting longer than you need to. **Anger needs to be kept under control!**

Psalm 37:8 Cease *from anger, and forsake wrath: fret not thyself in any wise to do evil.*

Proverbs 14:17 He (or she) that is soon angry dealeth foolishly: and a man (or woman) of wicked devices is hated.

These two verses tell us, to turn away from anger and that anger is foolish. I know this area of a broken relationship is tough and hard to overcome, but be Christ like. When you feel anger in your heart, you need to start to pray, don't let satan play with your mind or your life.

1: Anger: a strong feeling of grievance and displeasure, to become or make somebody extremely annoyed.

    a: disagree
    b: strongly disagree
    c: agree
    d: strongly agree

2: Write out some of the ways anger makes you feel:_____
_____
_____
_____
_____
_____
_____
_____
_____
_____
_____

3: In all relationships the last thing you need is anger in the relationship or companionship. If you know you need to change, just change.

    a: true b: false

4: Anger can kill you and your health. Anger will cause you to sin and cause you great pain. Anger only hurts!

    a: disagree
    b: strongly disagree
    c: agree
    d: strongly agree

5: (fill in the blanks): **Psalm 37:8** Cease from _____, and forsake _____: fret not thyself in any wise to do_____ _____.

6: (fill in the blanks): **Proverbs 14:17** He (or she) that is soon_____ dealeth foolishly: and a man (or woman) of_____devices is _____ _____.

7: What can we learn from **Psalm 37:8?**

_____
_____
_____
_____
_____
_____
_____
_____
_____
_____
_____
_____
_____

8: What can we learn from **Proverbs 14:17?**

_____
_____
_____
_____
_____
_____
_____
_____

9: In order to change your anger level, you must control your emotions. This is the first place to start.

    a: disagree
    b: strongly disagree
    c: agree
    d: strongly agree

10: This is a question that I would like for you to take time in answering; have you been taught to have anger, either by yourself or family member, other people, or society?

    a: disagree
    b: strongly disagree
    c: agree
    d: strongly agree

11: What can you do to change your anger?_____

_____

_____

_____

_____

_____

_____

_____

_____

_____

_____

_____

Notes:_____

_____

_____

_____

_____

_____

_____

_____

_____

_____

NEVER LOVE ANYONE MORE THAN GOD

Please read this!

If we as single adults would only do what this title stated, this alone might keep us from getting into the wrong relationship or getting hurt. **My pastor and brother Dr. Ed Davis told me this right after a broken relationship** that left me with a broken heart. *He said, "Bill, never love anyone more than God our Father. Never!"* *Sin will keep you from God.* Sin is sin; this will make division between God and mankind! That's a fact you can bank on. **Dr. Davis was right and let me show you why!**

<u>1 John 4:19</u> *We love him (God our Father), because he first loved us.*

This is our first love. This is the love that heals; the love that hurts!

LOVE THAT HURTS = that person wasn't a friend / mistakes / hate / broken relationship / bad relationship / satan / sin

LOVE THAT HEALS = friend / love / forgiveness / understanding / peace / God our Father

It's when we take our eyes off of God, our Father, that will cause us to have a great fall in the flesh! Look up this Bible verse:

<u>1 John 5:7</u> *For there are three that bear record in heaven, the Father (God), the word (Jesus Christ), and the Holy Ghost (HOLY SPIRIT); and these three are one.*

When we keep our heart and eyes on God our Father, we have our first love. That is the greatest love known to mankind! I will speak openly here. *Marriage is a great thing in the eyes of God, our Father. Marriage is where two people become one in Covenant.* **That is the love we, as single adults, should work toward.**

What happens when we take our heart and eyes off of God, our Father? Flesh takes over!

FLESH = CARNAL

CARNAL: (Worldly), to give into the desires of the flesh; following their natural desires that leads the Christians into mistakes and sin.

What would happen, if you would live by the Ten Commandments? *I will speak for myself. I would not be as carnal, so* what would happen to you, if you kept the Ten

Commandments? What is love? We know that it is about God's being our first love. What is love? Let's turn to the next Bible verse:

2 John 2:4 *And this is love, that we walk after His commandments. This is the commandment. That, as ye have heard from the beginning, ye should walk in it.*

This is such a large verse. Let's look at this verse in parts: **1st part:** (and this is love), go back to **2 John 2:4 ... we have received a commandment from the Father (God).** What was the commandment from God? We can find that answer in Exodus 20: 1-17 (The Ten Commandments). But let's look at **Exodus 20: 1 *And God spake all these words saying. (God spoke these Ten Commandments)!* 2nd part:** That we walk after his commandments. (What are we doing if we are walking toward his commandments?) We are walking in his love not ours! If we walk after his commandments, it is a narrow road. Look at the book of Matthew

Mathew 7: 13-14 *Enter ye in at the strait gate: for wide is the gate, and broad is the way, that leadeth to destruction, and many there be which go in thereat: Vs. 14: Because strait is the gate, and narrow is the way, which leadeth unto life, and few there be that find it.*

3rd part: That, as ye have heard from the beginning, ye should walk in it. (God spoke all these words saying).

John 14:15 *If ye love me, keep my commandments.*

God gave the Ten Commandments as a gift that would keep us on the narrow road. In my life, when I walked off this narrow road it always led to destruction. Well you might say, "Now brother, we are not under the law of the Ten Commandments." No, that isn't what I am saying. We should live with the Ten Commandments as we live with God. For God did speak these words. But more so, if we would live with these, Ten Commandments, life would be more of a blessing then the Hell we live in. Don't you think?

So never love anyone more than God our Father; this will help prevent you from getting into a bad relationship or the troubles of life!

1: (fill in the blanks) 2 John 2:4 And this is _____, that we walk after His_____. This is the commandment. That, as ye have heard from the beginning, ye should walk in it.

2: In your own words what does **John 14:15** mean to you? _____

_____

_____

_____

_____

_____

_____

_____

_____

_____

_____

_____

_____

3: So never love anyone more than God, our Father, this will help you from getting into a bad relationship or the troubles of life!

    a: disagree
    b: strongly disagree
    c: agree
    d: strongly agree

4: Write out what has happened to you when you did not put God's love first in a past relationship:

_____

_____

_____

_____

_____

_____

_____

_____

_____

_____

_____

_____

_____

_____

_____

_____

_____

_____

_____

RELATIONSHIP COMMITMENT

What does the word "commitment" mean to you and others? What has happened to this word in your real life relationships? Have you come to the point in your life where the word "commitment" means little when speaking about relationship? **Does our commitment (now) include trading people to get what we want?** People have been creating fake relationships for too long. Now they have false commitments just to please themselves. This is the reason for divorces, broken relationships, and is why they have increased throughout the years. Let me prove this. *How many false relationships have you been in?* **Maybe too many to count!**

People can't stay committed for more than a few months. What is going on with this? Let's take a look at this word.

Commitment: *to put into charge or trust: entrust, to pledge or assign to some particular course or use.*

But this generation of men and women can't keep its entrusted pledges. If this is the real problem, why are we allowing ourselves to be torn apart from relationship commitments? When you are in a relationship without commitments, you may well be wasting your time and setting yourself up to be hurt. You are investing your heart and time in the wrong person. This is a foolish mistake.

You may be in a relationship where one would say, "Friends only!" It's when two people touch or have sex that brings forth the hurt. ***Since when has friendship hurt or caused people to use each other?***

So, this generation doesn't live with real commitments. Why? The Bible makes it so clear. The Bible states that at the end times, we would live like mankind did in the days of Noah. We have accepted the ways of our sinful lust to fill ourselves with sin. This is our choice, and we have no one else to blame.

One would ask, "Is it just the People, Church, or satan that has caused us to live without commitments."

Has the Church fallen away? The Church has not fallen away! But I feel they could do a better job in ministering to the single adults. The church needs to step up here and teach single adults who you are in Christ. The church needs to teach the real value of commitments to single adults who are working toward marriage, not broken relationships or broken marriages. This is where we build families. Without families we have no church. The family supports the church. Being single in a church will allow a church to grow, if we teach commitment toward marriage.

Without commitments, we are disrupting God's plans! This is why churches need to open their doors to single adult ministry. This will help keep the church alive and growing. **Single adults are one of the signs of a growing church.**

Does satan have a part in our lifestyle of no commitments?

Only if you allow him! You have a God given right as Christians (children of God) to run satan you of our relationships. I say that because we know what to expect from the devil and what God has given us. Satan can only operate as much as you allow him to. You need to kick satan out of your life. How can you do this? Don't open the door to temptation. If you do, you have allowed satan and all of his fallen angels to tempt you and the one you're trying to have a relationship with. Sexual temptation has been the fall of mankind. *I want to state this: satan does not have control over you, if you are a child of God.* Yes, you have sin in your life from time to time. We are not perfect! That is why you should repent. Walk in the way of Christ. The influence and temptation that Satan has on this world is real. That is why you need to be a Christian and live life as a Christian.

We need our men to be spiritual leaders and women to be spiritual as well! What about the flesh (men and women) factor?

Where is the real blame for this type of life style (no commitment)? Why are we having relationships without real commitments? It's not the Church! The temptation from satan is just a little part of this, if you are a real Christian! What about Hollywood? No, it's not Hollywood either! **It's because we are not walking in the spirit of God. The truth is when men stopped being the spiritual leaders and women stopped their spiritual walk with God, the relationships lost their commitments.** Mankind is to blame for this. This is why you don't have real commitments! *I've said this a thousand times and I'm going to say this again, "**People who fall in love (in a short time) for the most part will fall out of love. This was and is a fake relationship without real commitments. People who grow in love (taking their time) have a real foundation of love. This is where you see real commitments.**"* You have free will to be good or bad. To walk in sin or not to walk in sin, **these choices are made on a human level! It's up to you!** Commitments should be real and kept. For this is the will of God, our Father. In keeping your commitments, God will bless you and reward you. Only foolish people break commitments. You all know what happens to foolish people. The Bible makes it clear.

The truth is, you should keep your commitments alive in the spirit of God! When you want something you have never had. You have got to do something you have never done!
This is why we must live in a committed relationship!
John 13:17 *If ye know these things, happy are ye if ye do them.*

80

1: Commitment: to put into charge or trust: entrust, to pledge or assign to some particular course or use.

    a: disagree
    b: strongly disagree
    c: agree
    d: strongly agree

2: Have we come to the point in our human life where the word "commitment" is just a disposable relationship?

    a: disagree
    b: strongly disagree
    c: agree
    d: strongly agree

3: We have established false commitments just to please ourselves. These are the reason for divorces, broken relationships, and this is why they have increased throughout the years.

    a: disagree
    b: strongly disagree
    c: agree
    d: strongly agree

4: Let me prove question three. How many false relationships have you been in?

    a:1 -2 b: 3-4 c: 5-6 d: none

5: In your own words, what creates a false relationship?_____

_____
_____
_____
_____
_____
_____
_____
_____
_____
_____
_____

6: When you are in a relationship without commitments, you may well be wasting your time and setting yourself up to be hurt.

    a: disagree
    b: strongly disagree
    c: agree
    d: strongly agree

7: So this generation doesn't live with real commitments. Why? _____

_____

_____

_____

_____

_____

_____

_____

_____

_____

_____

_____

8: Being single in a church will allow a church to grow if we teach commitment toward marriage. Without commitments, we are disrupting with God's plans!

    a: true b: false

9: Does Satan have a part in our lifestyle of no commitments?

    a: true b:false

10: We have a God given right as Christians to run Satan out of our relationships. I say that because we know what to expect from the devil and what God has given us. Satan can operate only as much as you allow him to.

    a: disagree
    b: strongly disagree
    c: agree
    d: strongly agree

11: We need our men to be spiritual leaders and the women to be spiritual as well!

    a: disagree
    b: strongly disagree
    c: agree
    d: strongly agree

12: "People who fall in love (in a short time) for the most part will fall out of love. This was and is a fake relationship, without real commitments. People who grow in love (taking their time) have a real foundation of love. This is where you see real commitments."

   a: disagree
   b: strongly disagree
   c: agree
   d: strongly agree

13: The truth is you should keep your commitments alive in the spirit of God! In your own words write out why this is.

_____

_____

_____

_____

_____

_____

_____

_____

_____

_____

_____

_____

KEEPING YOUR COMMITMENT

When you search for your soul mate, what are you really looking for? In the chapter I wrote called "Relationship Commitment" I brought out that people don't keep their commitments. I showed you what causes a divorce, in another section. But I want to back you up to the start of your looking for your soul mate.

Most people are not even taught in this modern time that marriage should be for life. Let me open your heart and mind with a few questions.

1: Do you think that marriage should last forever?

    a: disagree
    b: strongly disagree
    c: agree
    d: strongly agree

2: Have you ever heard of companionship love and should you be taught this?

    a: disagree
    b: strongly disagree
    c: agree
    d: strongly agree

3: Can you explain love?

    a: yes b: no

4: Will you allow love to change you?

    a: disagree
    b: strongly disagree
    c: agree
    d: strongly agree

5: How many changes do you think you will go through in a marriage relationship?

    a: just a few
    b: some
    c: a lot
    d: none

6: Will you keep God's plan for marriage?

    a: yes b: no

7: How much time per day are you willing to pray for your marriage?

    a: 1 to 2 minutes
    b: 3 to 5 minutes
    c: once a day
    d: a few times per day

8: Can you understand that love brings forth forgiving?

    a: disagree
    b: strongly disagree
    c: agree
    d: strongly agree

9: Do you know that without a home church, you are setting your marriage up for failure?

    a: disagree
    b: strongly disagree
    c: agree
    d: strongly agree

10: You must learn to set goals together in order to have a vision or direction of life in your marriage; are you willing to do this?

    a: disagree
    b: strongly disagree
    c: agree
    d: strongly agree

11: Will you have to keep love and romance alive in your companionship?

    a: disagree
    b: strongly disagree
    c: agree
    d: strongly agree

12: Are you willing to do things before you have to be asked?

    a: disagree
    b: strongly disagree
    c: agree
    d: strongly agree

13: If you are the husband, are you going to be the spiritual leader?

    a: disagree
    b: strongly disagree
    c: agree
    d: strongly agree

14: If you are the wife, are you going to be the help mate?

    a: disagree
    b: strongly disagree
    c: agree
    d: strongly agree

15: What about when it comes to house and yard work, can both of you plan to keep a clean and sound home?

    a: disagree
    b: strongly disagree
    c: agree
    d: strongly agree

16: Will it be important to you to do things for your spouse before he or she asks?

    a: disagree
    b: strongly disagree
    c: agree
    d: strongly agree

17: Can you give quality time when needed to your spouse?

    a: disagree
    b: strongly disagree
    c: agree
    d: strongly agree

18: Should you be involved in your spouse's hobbies or activities?

    a: disagree
    b: strongly disagree
    c: agree
    d: strongly agree

19: Do you believe you should learn how to do all the different types of housework?

    a: disagree
    b: strongly disagree
    c: agree
    d: strongly agree

20: Is marriage a team effort?

    a: disagree
    b: strongly disagree
    c: agree
    d: strongly agree

21: If marriage is a team effort, are you going to understand that you may have to pick up the marriage to get it moving?

    a: disagree
    b: strongly disagree
    c: agree
    d: strongly agree

These are only a few questions and issues that you will have to face, learn and work through. **Relationships are always moving.** If you are a lazy person or self centered, you will not do your part. If your marriage is not worth all the effort it takes to keep the marriage alive, what good is it for you to be married? There is a lot of faith in these questions. Do you have faith?

I want us to take a close look at two words that people use in marriage and choose the one that fits God's plan for marriage. You need to be truthful here in selecting the word that should be used in marriage. Here are the two words: **union or unity**.

Do you want to have a marriage with a **union** between the two of you (man and woman)? Do you want this **union** to be for a lifetime? Is having a **union** strong enough to keep a commitment in your marriage? Is your companionship worth this **union**?

Do you want to have a marriage with **unity** between the two of you (man and woman)? Do you want this **unity** to be for a lifetime? Is having **unity** strong enough to keep a commitment in your marriage? Is your companionship worth this **unity**?

Okay, I used these two words **(union / unity)** with the same question, so I could bring out the facts. Which word have you chosen from these two examples? Be honest in this answer; the truth will always inform you and change you before it will set you free. Take your time in understanding this.

I want you to encourage your pastor and companion to talk about these two words.

By now, you may be thinking, what's the difference? I guess it is time to show you something that has been left out of companionship and marriage. But before I do, which of the two words have you chosen? Is it union or unity? One of these two words is a part of God's plan for marriage. This is a clue. You would have learned this if you had marriage counseling with a pastor of your home church! This is the 2 second clue. Do you think you should be in a union with God, or do you think you should be in unity with God? This is the 3 third clue, *so is it union or unity that you want in your companionship or marriage?*

Question:

What makes union in a marriage? _____
_____
_____
_____
_____
_____

What makes unity in a marriage? _____
_____
_____
_____
_____
_____

Union: The act of joining together: the act of joining together people or things to form a whole. Result of joining together: a result of joining together people or things. The word union is always attached to a legal or contract agreement that binds you as you join. Union is full of by-laws.

God is the same yesterday, today, and tomorrow. Do you think you could have a union with God? Union is always attached with legal issues that bind us. So it's a man-made plan to join together people who agree to be in a union. Remember, when you are in a union, you are just one person not two that becomes one. Do you think God will allow union in a marriage? What rules are in marriage? Are these rules man's or God's? If they were men, this would be a union. I want to share with you that God is not a union. God is God Almighty. God planned marriage, and thought of marriage before mankind did. You can read this in the book of Genesis. If you are seeking a soul mate and marriage, you should understand this.

Unity: Condition of being one: the state or condition of being one. Combination into one: the combining or joining of separate things or entities to form one. Something whole: something whole or complete, formed by combining or joining separate things or entities.

Harmony: harmony of opinion, interest, or feeling. Number one: mathematics; a number by which a given element of a mathematical system can be multiplied with the result being equal to the value of the given element.

God is and has always been about unity. When Jesus said, "My father and I are one" He was stating a unity structure of love. God created man, then God created woman for man to have someone to love. Unity is always about love and peace. Unity is never bondage. Unity is where two people become one; this is God's plan for marriage.

If your marriage is a union, then there are two people enforcing rules and by-laws that are created by one another to counter-offer each other of their needs, wants and desires. This is not the responsibility of love! This is the legal part of a marriage that is union-minded!

There is no counter offer in marriage or companionship love. There should only be unity of love, peace, and God's plans for marriage. If you step outside of this, it will become a union that will dissolve into hate and divorce!

There is only one thing that causes a divorce
it is when you leave God out of the unity of marriage.
A marriage without God is dead.
A marriage without God has no faith, vision, companionship, and no peace!
A marriage without a home church is headed down a road that leads to Hell!
I want you to read this next statement, make a copy of this to place this in the picture
frame of your mind. Carry this with you as you walk along life's roads. You will see the
effect this has when you hear about another divorce.

Union is not Unity.
When God is a part of the Union,
then it becomes unity!
A marriage without God is a Union of two people,
but not a Unity
Because God is left out!

Divorce is the next thing to death; it hurts all who are a part of this marriage. Between the in-laws and your family members; they will all feel and see the effects of a divorce. You are not the only one who will hurt over this issue. I will always believe that a divorce was made in Hell. A divorce is nothing more than pure Hell on earth. ***A divorce will destroy the value of love and peace!***

Let me prove this: It can take years to recover from a divorce. This includes finances, emotion, depression; your children will be affected by this (they will go astray) and the other family members. The one who cause the divorce will lead a life of unhappiness, loss of peace, stress, and bad health; you see, Satan has come to kill, steal, and destroy. When you seek or cause a divorce, you have just opened the door to Satan and his plans to destroy your family!

Satan and divorces;
Have no unity with God!

Write out what you think causes divorces:_____

_____

_____

_____

_____

_____

_____

_____

_____

_____

_____

_____

_____

_____

_____

_____

_____

_____

_____

_____

_____

_____

_____

_____

_____

AGE GROUP

This is another area of marriage in which people make mistakes. I will never understand this issue. People who marry someone else out of their age group are setting themselves up for a hard road in their marriage.

Here is a trend that I see after a divorce, some men will marry a younger woman who is way out of their age group. From the start of this relationship, it is about pleasing themselves! The woman may be looking for a "sugar daddy' or "money daddy", or she has been conned mentally into this. ***If your parents, pastor, love ones, or best friend, talks to you about the issue of age group, please listen, because they took the time to care enough to look out for you with love!***

Age group:

18 to 28 years old: 5 years apart

29 to 39 years old: 5 to 7 years a part

After forty: no more than 7 - 10 years a part

These are not rules; but I'm here to share with you. If you step outside of these marriage age groups, there will be more issues in this type of marriage than you can realize.

Talk to your pastor about this issue. Most marriages that include people out of their age groups are because of one of these reasons, money, sex, feeling younger, gold digging, mentally conning, people using people as a property (like a slave or to have someone to show off like a pet), and so on!

People who marry out of their age group will often have other sexual relationships while married! They may be sex predators and may not have any understanding about love or marriage!

Write out how you feel about age group, when it comes to dating or marriage:

_____

_____

_____

_____

_____

_____

_____

PREDATORS WHO WANT TO BE MARRIED

for security, sex, or money

There are people who are taught by people in our society to marry for money, security, and / or sex. For the most part, this type of marriage is not of God's plan, and this type of marriage has no value of love. In a marriage that is for money, security or sexual desire, there is no companionship love.

This type of marriage is a union of marriage and has no unity. Most likely one of the two is or will become dominating. This will happen soon after the marriage! This type of marriage will have a problem from the get go. It will seem like a war that never ends; this is because there is no real love or trust. This type of marriage will make one of the two more a servant, than a soul mate.

Age may be a factor here. A rich man or woman, looking to feel young seeks to get someone younger than himself or herself. This type of predator makes his or her spouse a pet, rather than a person. This union is compromised with gifts or money in exchange for marriage. This compromised relationship is built on material issues and not love. Each one of the spouses is always in a state of wanting and never giving freely.

The one with the money thinks he or she has a right to do whatever he or she wants. Many go on trips, whether they are business or pleasure, without their spouse to engage in sexual affairs. They even have sexual playmates outside of their marriage.

Let me ask you something about trust. If a person is married, and you know that this person is cheating on his or her spouse, how can you say this is a good person? If someone cannot be true and faithful to the person he or she is married to, how could you trust him or her on any issue? These types of people are living just for themselves, and they do not care who they harm or hurt in the walk of life.

Those people who seek this type of marriage are labeled as "Gold Diggers." This type of person, for the most part are weak-minded. They never knew love and are just as selfish as predators. They are like cry babies, and they are only satisfied when they are compensated with gifts and money. They have no understanding of unity and will believe or act in any way to keep a union of marriage. The treasure of their heart is materially built on whatever they can get out of every marriage. They do not know God's plan for marriage, and they are very hard to live with.

This type of person cannot be trusted. This type of person always seeks attention and always wants someone to feel sorry for them. They do not grow up as adults or mature. They never seek the wisdom that only God can give in a marriage.

These types of people will never seek God until they have faced the truth about themselves. This will take many years to learn to develop. Love is something that is learned from the beginning. From birth does one seek love! But we are developed in the sight of our parents. If your parents didn't love each other, you will not grow up to understand love. You will only understand how to fight, argue, not work as a union, and not have a full understanding of marriage. But there is hope when we allow God to give us understanding as a Christian. God does have a family that is full of love. Study your Bible to see Gods' plan of love and marriage.

Notes:

_____

_____

_____

_____

_____

_____

_____

_____

_____

_____

_____

_____

_____

_____

_____

_____

_____

_____

_____

_____

_____

_____

_____

_____

_____

COMPANIONSHIP

Couples in unity with companionship love

Oneness with their faith and love

May God bless us in all of our years to come

Putting our hearts together to make a home

Affection and love that will never end

I always want you to be my best friend

Oh, I have every day to show you I care

Now that we have each other there is no fear

She and I have an everlasting relationship

Here we stand in love of our companionship

In our hearts rest faith, love and trust

Prayers that keep our love from turning to dust

ASKING SOMEONE OUT ON A DATE

It all starts with respect, as I get into this writing I want to reveal my past experiences.

Is it okay for either the man or woman to ask out the other person? We should be able to understand that it is okay for a woman to ask out a man. I want to share with you ways of asking a person out.

1: **Asking someone out and not knowing him or her:** This, for the most part is unlikely to happen! Example: you walk up to someone who you do not know at all and ask him or her out. What do you think is going to happen? For the most part, you might get a small conversation with a big "no". But this might be a chance to ask for an e-mail or get his or her phone number, or give them yours. Timing is a friend here; allow him or her to contact you. Ask with a small statement of respect and move on.

2: **You slightly know a person who you want to ask out:** Like someone you go to school with, someone's friend, someone you have talked with a few times, or a co-worker. At least he or she has seen you and even may have spoken with you. I suggest that you give him or her, your phone number or e-mail address. Timing is a friend here, allow them to contact you. Ask with a small statement of respect and move on, unless he or she wants to have a conversation. Do not allow yourself to be overbearing or arrogant. This is a great time just for small talk. Once again, allow him or her to contact you.

3: **Someone asks you out just to have something to do:** I say, "Why not?" You do not have to set boundaries here. This is a chance to make a friend. It's okay for a man and a woman to be friends without dating. When we say "friends only", what are we saying? Just allow yourselves to be friends. This may just stay at the level of friendship and nothing more. If you are going out just as friends, this will give the two of you a chance to meet other people. Again, respect is needed here.

4: **Asking someone out you know:** This is a good place to start, for he or she already knows you. I want you to realize that he or she may say no. If this happens, do not ask why; this will show a sign of respect. Who knows, in time he or she may ask you out, if he or she know you. You do not have to give out your e-mail or phone number. If you think it's okay to do so, give him or her, your e-mail or phone number. Write on a piece of paper and keep your conversation small. Walk away and allow him or her space. If he or she wants to talk, do so as a friend only, and whatever you do, don't put him or her on the spot with your questions!

5: **Someone asked you out:** Respect is needed here. If you are seeing someone, address this and allow him or her to know with kindness. If you do not want to date, let him or her know with kindness. If you never want to go out with him or her, address this with much kindness and keep it short. If someone keeps asking you out and he or she does not get the message, explain with a stiffer statement. If you want to go out with him or her, get his or her e-mail or phone number. Have a few conversations with him or her and allow time to be a friend; just to get to know him or her. Why not?

6: **If someone is stalking you, take a real notice of this:** I'm speaking as a man; who will protect people. If someone is stalking you, there is a real issue going on here. You can handle it in a few ways. If you are in a public area, address him or her, I would ask that you ask someone to be a witness to this. Most people are willing to help you. If you are in a store, ask for management.

If you are alone, do not address this issue unless you have to. Another way is to take a friend along with you and address this with respect.

I really feel that you should call the Police Department and share with them that this is going on; you can ask if they would send out an officer to talk with him or her without filing charges. If you feel threatened, allow the Police Department to handle this issue; they will also advise you in what to do. If it is at this point; do what you think is right in protecting yourself!

7: **Someone tells you he or she does not want to go out with you: Leave him or her alone! No is still no. Do not ask him or her any more questions; walk away with respect. Do not give him or her your phone number or e-mail address.**

8: **Asking someone out at the work place:** This can be a big issue. I suggest you speak softly and with a low voice, so that other people cannot here you. This could embarrass the other person, but it still shows signs of respect. Do not make too much small talk; just leave him or her your phone number or e-mail. This is where time could be a real friend; allow him or her to contact you!

Notes:

_____

_____

_____

_____

_____

_____

_____

_____

_____

WHAT CAUSES A DIVORCE

God authorized the unity of marriage. ***Therefore if God is not your first love, how can you truly understand love!*** Without God, we are only walking in the flesh. Without God, you don't have the Holy Spirit. If you don't have the Holy Spirit, you don't have the spirit of God in and around you. You have power in the Holy Spirit! Believe this; you will need the Holy Spirit when the devil comes to destroy your marriage. *So, without being a Christian, how can you love or have power to keep your marriage together?* Let's look at what the word "flesh" means:

FLESH: A word for human contrast to the spirit (Matthew 26:41). The word is also used for unredeemed human nature and carnal appetites or desires which can lead to sin (Galatians 5:16, 17).

The first thing that happens before a DIVORCE, there is a break down in unity. Without God in your marriage, you are standing alone inside of your marriage. Without God, how can your marriage stand in **UNITY?** The devil seeks out to destroy marriages. It's been said, and I really believe, that the devil will attack the unity of the family before he attacks the unity of the church. You can see the effects of divorce in this country. Just about half or more marriages and 54% of Christian marriages today end in divorce! Without God as our first love, the unity of marriages may be on a path to be **DESTROYED.** Without **GOD,** how can your marriage stand the test of time? The foremost reason for divorces: **MARRIAGE WITHOUT GOD.** (When you leave God out of your life and marriage, you are giving the devil a foothold and control of your lives.) Take out your **BIBLE** and turn to the book of REVELATION. I want to show you a verse about the devil and satan:

REVELATION 12:9 *And the great dragon was cast out that old serpent, called the devil, and satan, which deceiveth the whole world: he was cast out into the earth, and his angels were cast out with him.*

Here, in this verse in Revelation, you see that the devil and his angels were cast into the earth to deceive the whole earth and mankind! Now, you are in a real test without God. Not only must you stand against the devil, there are also his fallen angels. Do you think you can take on the devil and his angels without God in your life or marriage? Let's take a look at another verse:

1 PETER 5:8 *Be sober, be vigilant; because your adversary the devil, as a roaring lion, walketh about, seeking whom he may devour:*

The adversary, the devil, along with his ***fallen angels***, are seeking whom he (they) may devour! Does this include you? Yes, it does! That's why you need God in your life and to be a **REAL CHRISTIAN.** Let's look at the words "devour", "sober" and "vigilant":

DEVOUR: to bring to an end by or as if by the action of a destroying force.

SOBER: SENSIBLE, TEMPERATE AND SELF-CONTROLLED: this is an appropriate attitude for believers, as we await the Lord's return.

VIGILANT: paying close attention usually with a view to anticipating approaching danger or opportunity.

How much more of a reason do you need, than these last two verses? You need to have and keep God as your first love! You must keep and have God's unity in your marriage, familyand churches! When you take God out of the unity structure of marriage; the devil will try to devour your marriage, family or your Christian life!

"Union is not unity" unless God is a part of the union!
"A marriage without God is a Union of two people, but not a unity, because God is left out!"

UNITY: continuity without deviation or change (as in purpose or action of God's plans).

With this understanding of unity, we can see the effect it can have on marriages. Now, think about people you know who are divorced. Remember, there is no unity without God! This means you are standing alone to fight the devil and his fallen angels alone. What happens to marriage without God? What will happen to marriages and families without the unity of God? Now, we can see the effects of marriages and family without God and without God's unity. No wonder marriages and families are being destroyed. *We blame everything on the reasons that cause all these divorces. But, we still leave out God, WHY? Now that you see what causes divorces, will you marry without God? Now you know the truth about divorces!*

1: God authorized the unity of marriage.

    a: disagree
    b: strongly disagree
    c: agree
    d: strongly agree

2: **FLESH:** A word for human contrast to the spirit (Matthew 26:41). The word is also used for unredeemed human nature and carnal appetites or desires which can lead to sin (Galatians 5:16, 17).

a: disagree
b: strongly disagree
c: agree
d: strongly agree

3: The first thing that happens before a DIVORCE, there is a break down in unity.

a: disagree
b: strongly disagree
c: agree
d: strongly agree

4: The foremost reason for divorces: MARRIAGE WITHOUT GOD.

a: disagree
b: strongly disagree
c: agree
d: strongly agree

5: In your own words, why did you choose your answer concerning question four?

_____
_____
_____
_____
_____
_____
_____
_____
_____
_____
_____
_____
_____

6: (please fill in the blanks): **1 PETER 5:8** Be _____, be _____ _____; because your _____ the _____ ___, as a roaring _____, walketh about, _____ whom he may: _____.

7: What does "devour" mean to you? _____

_____
_____
_____
_____
_____
_____
_____
_____
_____
_____
_____
_____
_____

8: What does "sober" mean to you? _____

_____
_____
_____
_____
_____
_____
_____
_____
_____
_____
_____
_____
_____

9: What does "vigilant" mean to you? _____

_____
_____
_____
_____
_____
_____
_____
_____
_____
_____
_____
_____
_____

10: "Union is not unity" unless God is a part of the union (then it becomes unity)! "A marriage without God is a union of two people, but not a unity because God is left out!

    a: disagree
    b: strongly disagree
    c: agree
    d: strongly agree

11: Concerning question ten, why did you choose your answer? _____

_____

_____

_____

_____

A LOOK AT THE FOUR TEMPERAMENTS

I have listed the four types of temperaments from notations from my Pastor's teaching, so that you can take a look at them. There are tests that you can do on the internet, but ***I suggest having a certified counselor or Pastor to do this with you.***

I want everyone who reads this subject on temperaments to understand that I'm not a counselor, *but I decided to give you an insight to these four temperaments. I feel people do not understand who they are, or other people and this alone accounts for many broken relationships. If you do not match in your temperaments there is no one to blame and that includes yourself. I've kept this short and you can study this on your own. Temperament tests are used in marriage counseling.*

Temperaments: A prevailing or dominant quality of mind that characterizes someones, excessive moodiness, irritability, or sensitivity, and history in medieval physiology, the quality of the mind resulting from various proportions of the four cardinal humors in somebody.

Sanguine

The sanguine temperament is fundamentally impulsive and pleasure-seeking; sanguine people are sociable and charismatic. They tend to enjoy social gatherings, making new friends and tend to be boisterous. They are usually quite creative and often daydream. However, some alone time is crucial for those of this temperament. Sanguine can also mean sensitive, compassionate and romantic. Sanguine personalities generally struggle with following task, all the way through, are chronically late, and tend to be forgetful and sometimes a little sarcastic. Often, when they pursue a new hobby, they lose interest as soon as it ceases to be engaging or fun. They are very much people persons. They are talkative and not shy. Sanguine generally have an almost shameless nature, certain that what they are doing is right. They have no lack of confidence.

Sanguine- *The not so great Characteristics*

Vanity and self=complacency, loving the appearance of his/herself and the praise of others. The sanguine is very inclined to flirt, and has a great degree of jealous tendencies. The sanguine cannot be left alone. There is a cheerfulness and love of pleasure that accompany the desire to always have someone around to enjoy life with. The sanguine decisions are likely to be the wrong decisions, their undertaking fail easily since they believe success is inevitable and will therefore take it for granted, they are unstable, and they have little understanding of themselves since they rarely internalize conflict.

Choleric

The choleric temperament is fundamentally ambitious and leader-like. They have a lot of aggression, energy, and/or passion, and try to instill it in others. They can dominate people of other temperaments, especially phlegmatic types. Many great charismatic military and political figures were choleric. They like to be in charge of everything. However, cholerics also tend to be either highly disorganized or highly organized. They do not have in-between setups, only one extreme to another. As well as being leader-like and assertive, cholerics also fall into deep and sudden depression. Essentially, they are very much prone to mood swings.

Choleric -*The not so great Characteristics*

The choleric is commonly prideful, full of him/her, thinking highly of his/her great qualities and even considers his/her faults worthy of praise. also, is stubborn and has an opinion on everything. The choleric believes he/she is always right. The choleric is confident, believes others are weak, ignorant, incompetent and slow. Upon humiliation the choleric feels hurt resulting in anger, deceit, and judgments towards others.

Melancholic

The melancholic temperament is fundamentally introverted and thoughtful. Melancholic people often were perceived as very (or overly) pondering and considerate, getting rather worried when they could not be on time for events. Melancholics can be highly creative in activities such as poetry and art - and can become preoccupied with the tragedy and cruelty in the world. Often they are perfectionists. They are self-reliant and independent; one negative part of being a melancholic is that they can get so involved in what they are doing they forget to think of others.

Melancholic - *The not so great Characteristics*

Easily falls into mental distress and this can be extremely intense. The melancholic, more than any other temperament, has keen awareness of moral right and wrong, and has a deep longing for morality. They are inclined to despair, intense expressions of grief, and occurrences of depression. This can result in self-pity, and he/she may become a burden to friends and family. He/she can also lose confidence in others, specifically superiors; there is a loss of trust and respect when the melancholy becomes aware of a fellow man's weaknesses and faults. The melancholy vehemently desires justice, and forgiveness of offences is hardly an option. He/she is suspicious, lacks trust in people and fears that everyone is out to get him/her. He/she is pessimistic about everything.

Phlegmatic

The phlegmatic temperament is fundamentally relaxed and quiet, ranging from warmly attentive to lazily sluggish. Phlegmatics tend to be content with themselves and are kind. They are accepting and affectionate. They may be receptive and shy and often prefer stability to uncertainty and change. They are consistent, relaxed, calm, rational, curious, and observant, qualities that make them good administrators. They can also be passive-aggressive.

Phlegmatic- *The not so great Characteristics*

Inclined to things that require little to no effort, eating, drinking, is lazy, and neglects duties. Often misses opportunities, has no ambition and no aspirations in life.

What temperament are you and why?

_____
_____
_____
_____
_____
_____
_____
_____
_____
_____
_____
_____
_____

If your temperament does match up with someone else, is there anyone to blame and why?

_____
_____
_____
_____
_____
_____
_____
_____
_____
_____
_____

What did you learn from this subject on temperaments?

_____
_____
_____
_____
_____
_____
_____
_____
_____
_____
_____
_____
_____
_____
_____
_____
_____
_____
_____
_____
_____
_____
_____

We must meet in order to come to know each other.
There must be an attraction to go to the next steps.
One of the two will ask the other out.
We must allow time to pass to come to know each other.
We must develop a type of friendship fi rst,
in order to start trusting one another.
With time and trust we develop a greater trust and then a great friendship.
The trust that is grown from the friendship area,
will allow the time to grow in love.
As love grows so will a greater trust.
Courtship develops here.
It's through courtship that people tend to become engaged to be married.
Marriage comes after the time of relationship growth.
Before marriage the two of you
needs to receive counseling from a Pastor!
Pastors are a part of God's unity structure.
Without counseling we may become foolish!
The last thing you need as a spouse is a foolish marriage!
In marriage we have companionship love.
Companionship love develops and creates our soul mate!
This is done by God's unity structure of marriage.
This is where we get the word, soul

By: Bill Carter

"LOOKING FOR YOUR SOUL MATE"

IS A
RELATIONSHIP DEVELOPMENT WORK BOOK
DESIGN TO BE USED AT HOME, CHURCH,
AND IN GROUP TEACHINGS!
ALL QUESTIONS IN THIS BOOK CAN BE USED
AS DISCUSSION QUESTIONS.

IF YOU WOULD LIKE FOR US TO COME AND SPEAK
AT YOUR CHURCH OR MEETINGS.
Just write us.
PLEASE SEND your letters TO,
and
if you wish to support our
singles ministry program,
you can send your love gifts to:

BILL CARTER
PO BOX 1602
OWENSBORO KY 42302

THANK YOU FOR PURCHASING THIS BOOK!

WESTBOW
PRESS
A DIVISION OF THOMAS NELSON

HTTP://WWW.LOOKINGFORYOURSOULMATE.NET